KENNETH LONERGAN

PHILOSOPHICAL FILMMAKERS

Series editor: Costica Bradatan is a Professor of Humanities at Texas Tech University, USA, and an Honorary Research Professor of Philosophy at the University of Queensland, Australia. He is the author of *Dying for Ideas: The Dangerous Lives of the Philosophers* (Bloomsbury, 2015), among other books.

Films can ask big questions about human existence: what it means to be alive, to be afraid, to be moral, to be loved. The *Philosophical Filmmakers* series examines the work of influential directors, through the writing of thinkers wanting to grapple with the rocky territory where film and philosophy touch borders.

Each book involves a philosopher engaging with an individual filmmaker's work, revealing how it has inspired the author's own philosophical perspectives and how critical engagement with those films can expand our intellectual horizons.

Other titles in the series
Terrence Malick, Robert Sinnerbrink
Eric Rohmer, Vittorio Hösle
Werner Herzog, Richard Eldridge

Other titles forthcoming
Shyam Benegal, Samir Chopra
Christopher Nolan, Robbie Goh
Leni Riefenstahl, Jakob Lothe

KENNETH LONERGAN

Filmmaker and Philosopher

TODD MAY

BLOOMSBURY ACADEMIC
LONDON • NEW YORK • OXFORD • NEW DELHI • SYDNEY

BLOOMSBURY ACADEMIC
Bloomsbury Publishing Plc
50 Bedford Square, London, WC1B 3DP, UK
1385 Broadway, New York, NY 10018, USA

BLOOMSBURY, BLOOMSBURY ACADEMIC and the Diana logo are trademarks of Bloomsbury Publishing Plc

First published in Great Britain 2020

Copyright © Todd May, 2020

Todd May has asserted his right under the Copyright, Designs and Patents Act, 1988, to be identified as Author of this work.

For legal purposes the Acknowledgments on p. vi constitute an extension of this copyright page.

Cover image: Kenneth Lonergan © Everett Collection / Bridgeman Images

All rights reserved. No part of this publication may be reproduced or transmitted in any form or by any means, electronic or mechanical, including photocopying, recording, or any information storage or retrieval system, without prior permission in writing from the publishers.

Bloomsbury Publishing Plc does not have any control over, or responsibility for, any third-party websites referred to or in this book. All internet addresses given in this book were correct at the time of going to press. The author and publisher regret any inconvenience caused if addresses have changed or sites have ceased to exist, but can accept no responsibility for any such changes.

A catalogue record for this book is available from the British Library.

A catalog record for this book is available from the Library of Congress.

ISBN: HB: 978-1-3501-1206-3
PB: 978-1-3501-1207-0
ePDF: 978-1-3501-1205-6
eBook: 978-1-3501-1208-7

Series: Philosophical Filmmakers

Typeset by Newgen KnowledgeWorks Pvt. Ltd., Chennai, India

To find out more about our authors and books visit www.bloomsbury.com and sign up for our newsletters.

CONTENTS

Preface and Acknowledgments vi
A Note on the Films vii

1   Introduction 1

2   Irredeemable Suffering 13

3   Self-Deception 51

4   Normative Complexity 89

5   Lonergan and Philosophy: Taking Stock 129

Notes 157
Bibliography 165
Index 169

PREFACE AND ACKNOWLEDGMENTS

I am grateful to Costica Bradatan for inviting me to contribute to Bloomsbury's *Philosophical Filmmakers* series and for encouraging me to write the book even against my protests that I am not a philosopher of film. I am also grateful to an anonymous reviewer for helpful suggestions and to Liza Thompson for shepherding the book through the press. It has been a pleasure to immerse myself in the films of Kenneth Lonergan and in the reflections to which this immersion has given rise. My colleague Chris Grau, as always, has been a generous and thoughtful conversational partner. In this case especially, since one of his areas of specialization is philosophy of film, he has guided me in particularly helpful ways. I hope I have not muddled his teaching too badly in my own approach to the cinematic questions that are raised here. My wife Kathleen read the entire manuscript and offered invaluable feedback along the way. I dedicate this book to her, David, Rachel, and Joel. They daily offer me reasons to believe; as Lonergan writes in *The Waverly Gallery*, "it must be worth a lot to be alive."

A NOTE ON THE FILMS

I used DVDs for the three films discussed here:

1. *You Can Count on Me*, from Paramount Classics and Hart Sharp Entertainment, produced in association with Cappa Productions. Director and Screenwriter: Kenneth Lonergan. Copyright: 2000, Paramount Classics. Among its special features is a voice-over commentary by Lonergan, which I refer to in the text and list in the bibliography.

2. *Margaret*, from Fox Searchlight Pictures and Camelot Pictures, produced by Gilbert Films/Mirage Enterprises/Scott Rudin. Director and Screenwriter: Kenneth Lonergan. Copyright: 2011, 2013, 2014, Twentieth Century Fox Film Corporation. This is the extended cut, which is discussed in the first chapter.

3. *Manchester by the Sea*, from Amazon Studios, produced by Pearl Street Films, The Media Farm, K Period Media, The A/Middleton Project B Story. Director and Screenwriter: Kenneth Lonergan. Copyright: 2016, K Films Manchester LLC. Among its special features is a conversational voice-over commentary with Lonergan, which I refer to in the text and list in the bibliography.

1

Introduction

We live in an artistic moment when the line between what is often called "high" culture and what is often called "popular" culture is being increasingly blurred. Novels such as those of David Foster Wallace and Haruki Murakami, television series like the Icelandic *Trapped*, the British *Broadchurch*, and the American *The Wire*; graphic works like Nick Drnaso's *Sabrina* and Maximilian Uriarte's *The White Donkey*; films of directors like Asghar Farhadi and Richard Linklater; and even a sitcom series like *The Good Place*—all of these offer themes, orientations, and rhetorics that can be appreciated as popular entertainment while at the same time inviting us to consider weightier issues traditionally associated with high culture.

This is not to deny that there may be other artists in other periods who blurred the line between "high" and "popular" culture, nor that there aren't works that fall clearly on one side or another of that line. Regarding the latter, movies like *Transformers* and television shows such as *SpongeBob SquarePants* are pretty clearly devoid of themes that might characterize them as contributants to "high" culture, whereas much work that falls into the category of philosophy seems destined for venues entirely outside the popular mind. As for the former, one can think of various artists such as Bach, Dickens, and perhaps even Giotto as exemplifying ways of approaching art that go beyond the entertainment usually considered as its central characteristic.

What seems to be special about the current climate is that we inhabit a period in which this blurring is particularly true across many artistic practices. It is a moment to which the films of Kenneth Lonergan offer an important contribution. Although, as of this writing, he has directed only three films, they can all be watched as movies that appeal to wider audiences (*You Can Count on Me* and *Manchester by the Sea* both garnered Oscar nominations) at the same time that they offer, as we shall see, significant philosophical contributions to understanding important aspects of our lives.

One might want to balk here at this characterization of our cultural moment, particularly with regard to film. Wasn't the period that included auteurs like Godard, Fellini, Bergman, and others also one that crossed "popular" with "high" culture? I think of it otherwise. It seems to me that the stakes of that period were less the blurring of boundaries than an attempt to take an artistic practice that had traditionally been associated with mass entertainment and show that it offered the possibility of producing works of "high" culture. Many of the films coming from the most respected directors of the period from the 1950s and 1960s are difficult to watch as entertainment; instead they are experiments in filmmaking that seek to push the boundaries of what the cinematic experience can be. (By entertainment here, I do not mean simply fun but more broadly accessibility to a wider audience.) Nevertheless, even if we insist on calling that period or another one a blurring of boundaries between "high" and "popular" culture, it is surely the case that we are living in one now, and across a variety of arts. And it is just as sure that Lonergan's work sits squarely within this movement of blurring.

Lonergan himself began his career not as a director, nor even as someone associated with film. He was originally allied to the theater. (Many of the details of Lonergan's life recounted here are drawn from Rebecca Mead's important *New Yorker* profile, "The Cinematic Triumphs of Kenneth Lonergan.")[1] He grew up in New York and started writing in the fifth grade. When he was 18 he won a competition at the Young Playwright's Festival. For college he went to New York's University's dramatic writing program, soon joining a downtown theater company called Naked Angels. Although some of the material that was developed for Naked Angels found its way into his later cinematic work, more immediately it generated a commitment to the theater. His first full-length play, *This Is Our Youth*, premiered in 1996 and eventually garnered very positive reviews. He has since written six other plays in addition to the screenplays for the films *Analyze This*, *Analyze That*, *Gangs of New York*, and for the recent television remake of *Howard's End*. Although the focus here will be on the three films Lonergan directed, his theatrical background is important for understanding the films themselves, for two reasons.

First, there is a theatrical feel to the films. The focus is on the characters and situations in the films rather than on special effects or other formal elements. Although we will periodically see the use of formal elements in the films—usually thematic indicators of one sort or another—they do not occupy nearly as important a place as the interpersonal relationships and unfolding characterizations he places before us. It would be a mistake to go so far as to claim that Lonergan's films are simply cinematically presented plays, although they are probably closer to that than most films that pass as entertainment.

The second reason has to do with the actors themselves. In the voice-over to *You Can Count on Me*, Lonergan notes that almost all of his actors come from the theater. Given his background this should not be surprising. Not only are his early connections developed in the theater, but he has remained an active playwright throughout his film career. Moreover, the skills he is looking for in actors for his films are those associated with the stage. He is less concerned with aspects of cinema that are peculiar to that medium and is instead more focused on theatrical skills. In addition, many of the actors recur across his films, such as Mark Ruffalo, Matthew Broderick, and his wife J. Smith-Cameron.

Another important influence in his cinematic work is the environment in which he grew up. Both of Lonergan's parents were practicing psychoanalysts. He joked to Rebecca Mead that he was "raised by the New York Psychoanalytic Society," explaining that discussion of patients was common dinner table talk. "Talking about people's personalities, and why people do things, is a big part of my life, and has been since I was little."[2] This account of his upbringing reinforces Lonergan's commitment to an approach to cinema that would be oriented toward the theater. It reveals something else as well.

As we will see, his characters have a depth and complexity that often goes missing in film characters. This is a central trait of Lonergan's characters, one that, I will argue throughout, has philosophical implications. Among the aspects of this depth is one associated with psychoanalysis: self-deception. Lonergan's characters are often acting out of motives of which they are unaware and would have reason not to bring to awareness. This is a core theme in psychoanalysis. The concepts of repression and the unconscious are posited by Freud largely to account for self-deception, and so exposure to the phenomenon undoubtedly appeared early in his life. Although we will distance ourselves here from the traditional psychoanalytic approach, we devote an entire chapter to the appearance of self-deception in his films.

To date, then, Lonergan has directed three films: *You Can Count on Me*, *Margaret*, and *Manchester by the Sea*, which appeared in 2000, 2011, and 2016, respectively. However, the date for *Margaret* is misleading. Behind this date is a story, recounted by Rebecca Mead in her profile of Lonergan, that helps explain why his output in the sixteen years after *You Can Count on Me* consists of only two films. *Margaret* was the subject of intense disagreement, leading to legal proceedings that left Lonergan bitter and depressed.

The film, which Lonergan sought to be his masterpiece, was shot in 2005, four years after he began writing it, and was ready to be shown the following year. In fact, he did show it to a few friends. The problem was that it was over three hours long. It originally had been far longer: three hundred and seventy-five pages in typescript. (Mead comments that this is three times the length of a standard script.) Lonergan told Mead that "I cut a hundred pages out of it without turning a hair, and then I cut another hundred pages of it without much difficulty, and then I stopped, because I wasn't sure if I was making the cuts that were good, or because I was trying to get it to a normal length."[3] That was where the trouble began.

Fox Searchlight, with whom Lonergan had contracted, demanded a version of the film that was no longer than two-and-a-half hours.

Eventually, in 2008, he gave them several cuts of the film, one of which met the length requirement. However, he was not at all happy with it. "We did one cut where we just shortened all the scenes, and it fell apart, completely and obviously."[4] So Lonergan kept working on the film, at a great personal and financial expense. At the same time, he was distancing himself from the shorter cut. Fox hired someone to do the cut for him, but he rejected it. Then he hired Martin Scorsese to work on a version, but, as Mead notes, "by that time, Gary Gilbert, one of the producers, was suing Lonergan, and Scorsese's version never saw the light of day."[5]

All of this drained Lonergan; moreover, when the film was finally released in 2011, six years after it was shot, it was the short version. And, to add insult to injury, it opened in just two theaters. The masterpiece that Lonergan had envisioned had been diminished and then forgotten. In addition, two years later the Gilbert lawsuit began, although it was soon dropped when Gilbert saw the list of Hollywood royalty lined up to testify on Lonergan's behalf. But the dispute had taken its toll. It was not until five years after the release of the short version of *Margaret* that another Lonergan film appeared: *Manchester by the Sea*, surely one of the most wrenching films to find its way onto a screen. (Fortunately for all of us, the longer version of *Margaret* is now available as an "extended" cut, since it is still legally not allowed to be called a "director's" cut.)

The poem after which the film is named, "Spring and Fall," is by Gerard Manley Hopkins. There is no character in the film named Margaret, but the poem itself is discussed in one of the English classes Lisa Cohen, the film's main character, attends. We will see it again in the following chapter, but here it is in full:

Márgarét, áre you gríeving
Over Goldengrove unleaving?
Leáves like the things of man, you
With your fresh thoughts care for, can you?
Ah! ás the heart grows older
It will come to such sights colder
By and by, nor spare a sigh
Though worlds of wanwood leafmeal lie;
And yet you wíll weep and know why.
Now no matter, child, the name:
Sórrow's spríngs áre the same.
Nor mouth had, no nor mind, expressed
What heart heard of, ghost guessed:
It ís the blight man was born for,
It is Margaret you mourn for.[6]

The poem can be seen as expressing, among other things, the sadness and regret that we experience as we grow older, a theme that is relevant to Lisa's unfolding journey. However, it can also be seen, in retrospect, to be relevant to the events surrounding the release of the film itself. Lonergan came to regret his actions with the studio. According to Mead, "Lonergan acknowledges that he was recalcitrant and difficult about 'Margaret'… The lesson that Lisa Cohen learns in the course of the movie—that she cannot bend intransigent forces to comply with her own sense of personal justice—mirrors Lonergan's struggle to see his artistic vision realized."[7] The poem "Margaret" does not refer to senses of personal justice, but it does convey a sense of regret that attends to both Lisa's actions (more particularly her participation in causing a death) and Lonergan's (less momentous but also less fictional) struggles with Fox.

Turning to the films themselves, there are, as with many intelligent films, a number of themes that could be discussed. Some of these will be woven into the discussion of the three themes we isolate here. What is of concern for us is the philosophical relevance of the films, and that will point us in specific directions, directions that cannot capture the entirety of any one of the films but that will allow us to see at least some of their philosophical relevance. We are fortunate in that there are only three films; this allows us to look more deeply into what is going on in them than we would be able to if we had to canvas a larger corpus.

Moreover, there is a single overarching theme that draws all three films together, or perhaps better a theme about which the films revolve in their different ways: that of death. In *You Can Count on Me*, the parents of the two siblings Samantha and Terry Prescott who are the focus of the film die at the outset. Underlying their particular struggles, in ways we will see, is the lingering haunting of that death. In *Margaret*, Lisa Cohen participates, along with a bus driver Gerald Maretti, in the accidental death of a pedestrian on a street in New York. Finally, in *Manchester by the Sea*, the main character, Lee Chandler, through a small act of neglect, causes his children to die in a fire. None of these deaths occur in the same way, and the relationship of these various characters to those deaths is particular to them. This, in fact, is part of the philosophical significance of the films. As we will see throughout, and will be discussed at more length in the concluding chapter, among the philosophical relevance of Lonergan's films is their undermining of several sweeping philosophical claims or orientations. By focusing on the complexity of his characters' relation to their situations and to one another, these films challenge simple philosophical formulas and invite us to see ourselves as more complicated than such formulas might lead us to believe.

The first of these complications involves a confrontation with an aphorism by the philosopher Friedrich Nietzsche. "*From life's military school*—what doesn't kill me makes me stronger" (emphasis in original).[8] It is spoken in the first person, but does not refer solely to the speaker. It is also not an aphorism that is restricted to the philosophical community. In one way or another it has found its way into our larger culture, and indeed into popular life. Moreover, it can stand as a way to frame an entire life, to think of a life—or life generally—as a series of confrontations with challenges that will either be vanquished or vanquish the challenged. Taken in this way, it is what might be called a stereotypical masculine view of life. Life is a test of your strength and resolve; man up.

There is, to be sure, a place where that aphorism might be apt. There are moments when it is inspiring to think of the struggles that await one as tests of will and purpose rather than simply burdens to be endured. At those moments one confronts oneself, demands that one meet the struggle face-to-face rather than resign oneself to the situation. But as exhortation to a way of living it is impoverished. It urges us to neglect important aspects of our emotional lives, those emotional aspects that involve fragility or vulnerability. Is the rejection by a lover, or the loss of a loved one, or the failure in an important project really nothing more than the opportunity to test one's will, to manifest steadfastness, or to overcome in the face of onslaughts?

Moreover, and this will be the theme of the following chapter, taken literally the aphorism is false. What doesn't kill me does not always make me stronger. This is not, as will be seen, because it always makes me weaker. There is, as Lonergan's films show, no "always" here. We are too complex, too multifarious, for that. What does not kill me may have any of a variety of effects on me, depending on who I am, what my circumstances are, and how I perceive that which is not exactly killing me.

The second complication addresses our understanding of self-deception. In philosophy there is a traditional paradox that needs to be resolved in thinking about self-deception. How can I deceive myself without knowing that I am doing so and thereby undermining the attempt? We will follow that paradox, see how it is resolved in the work of Sigmund Freud, and then turn to a different way of thinking about self-deception that is more adequate to the phenomenon. We will also see how Lonergan's films display this more adequate approach, how self-deception is rooted not only in an individual's psyche but also in the social world of which she is a part. And, as with Nietzsche's aphorism, it will appear as a more complicated phenomenon than we might be tempted to think.

In addition, and in contrast to common views of self-deception, in *Manchester by the Sea* Lonergan will show us that self-deception is not always a bad thing. The film's protagonist, Lee Chandler, is a paragon of the refusal of self-deception, but this does not help him cope with the tragedy that has befallen him.

The final complication involves what might be called "normative complexity." Standard philosophical moral theories offer idealized ways to act or to live. They can be useful in certain circumstances as normative guides. But they can also be misleading, and in three ways. First, such theories invite us to simple moral judgments about others, which are often myopic. We are, all of us, more than simply creatures to be judged on against one or another moral standard. There are, we might say, a number of ledgers for judgment, as well as reasons often to refrain from judgment at all, when we think of the complexity of our fellow human beings. To be sure, there might be times when moral judgment rightly rises above all other considerations, and when those moral judgments are straightforward. But these are the extreme instances; they do not form the ether of our everyday lives.

And if there are other ledgers aside from the moral one, there are other values aside from moral values that can be pursued or integrated into a life. What we admire in others or seek to be ourselves is not only moral uprightness. It might be spontaneity or charm, warmth or loyalty, curiosity or intensity. To be sure, there are reasons to hold as central in our pantheon of values the moral ones. Philosophers have long argued that they override all others. However, when we look at those around us with a more empathic eye we are likely to see people in a more nuanced light. Those who fall short on our moral scale may display other, nonmoral qualities that might merit our consideration, our affection, and even at times our admiration.

Finally, to make matters even more complicated, those who fall short on one measure of morality might be more adequate, or even excel, in another. Morality itself is not a single ledger by which to measure a person. It can involve values that are diverse and perhaps in specific situations in conflict with one another. Someone might be at once decent and indecent, depending on the moral lens through which she is seen, and this even without descending into some form of moral relativism. Decent in one way, indecent in another; morally admirable but still, in some fashion, morally deficient. Moral judgments of people, unlike judgments of action or personal traits, are rarely simple matters, although our moral theories may mislead us into thinking they are.

Lonergan's films, because they present us with people in their full complexity, wrest simple judgment from our grips. They also challenge simple philosophical formulations concerning strength, self-deception, and morality. They do so in situations that involve death and so bring people face-to-face with human extremity. Without reverting to abstraction or descending to pontification, while still remaining squarely within the realm that is often, if increasingly misleadingly, called "popular," *You Can Count on Me*, *Margaret*, and *Manchester by the Sea* leave us with a richer sense of humanity than we—and much of our philosophy—often recognize. We will see what lessons this offers for philosophy in the final chapter. But before that we will look at the specific challenges themselves. It is to that task that we now turn.

2

Irredeemable Suffering

Among Nietzsche's most famous aphorisms this one occupies a singular place: "What doesn't kill me makes me stronger."[1] It offers stirring words. It is a call to overcome self-pity, a goad to action, and a consolation to those who are in pain. If we meditate on this aphorism we might be able to confront obstacles that face us with greater determination or grit, not be cowed by what seem like insuperable odds, see past our own suffering toward what we might want to accomplish.

It is also false. We know this. (Whether Nietzsche himself believed it is another matter. In fact, the question of what Nietzsche believed is a vexed matter in scholarly interpretation. We will refer to the aphorism as "Nietzsche's aphorism" but not argue for it as a view Nietzsche endorsed or rejected, in order to maintain the potential distance between the two.)[2] What doesn't kill me does not always make me stronger. Not because it always makes me weaker. Instead what doesn't kill me may make me stronger, or weaker, or something else. And if it does make me stronger or weaker it might do so in any number of ways. It might make me more determined, or less. What does not kill me might make me more empathic with those who face obstacles of their own, or more callous toward them. It might offer me insight into myself that will be useful moving forward in my life, or it might block that insight. It might open me up to new experiences, or it might make me fearful of them. And depending on what "it" is and who I am, it might shatter my life without entirely killing me.

If we are to test Nietzsche's aphorism we might do so at the extreme: death. Not my own death, or your death, but the death of others. It could be the death of those we love, of friends or acquaintances, or even the death of strangers. Confronting one's own death involves a certain kind of suffering, the suffering of coming to terms with the end of the entirety of one's being, one's projects and relationships, as well as the small joys such as waking up from a nap and seeing the sun dapple the leaves on the tree outside the window. With the death of others it is different. One goes on, one is still here, but one's world has changed. It has become diminished somehow. That "somehow" is different depending not only on the relationship with the person who has died but also on the relationship to the death itself.

A central theme in Kenneth Lonergan's three films is the relation of death to suffering. However, to put it that way already renders the issue too abstract. There isn't *the* relation of death to suffering. There are various relations. He investigates three different deaths: the death of one's parents, the death one causes (or participates in causing) of a stranger, and the death one causes of one's children. But even that articulation is too abstract, and his films show us this. There are different ways these relations might unfold. If we are to be precise about it, we should put it this way. He investigates the relation of Terry Prescott and of Samantha Prescott to the death of their parents.

He investigates the relation of Lisa Cohen and Gerald Maretti to the death they have participated in causing of Monica Patterson, whom they did not know. And he investigates the relation of Lee Chandler (and to a lesser extent of Randy Chandler) to the death of his children, a death he has caused.

If we put the matter this way, however, then we must confront a philosophical challenge, one that emerges when we move from the abstract to the concrete. If the relationship of death to suffering—or, more generally, of what doesn't kill us to what happens to us—can be grasped only through the experiences of particular people, what lesson can there be for us? What do I learn from knowing that, for instance, Sammy Prescott dealt with her parents' death by trying to make sure everything around her was okay, nothing out of control, while her brother Terry introduced chaos wherever he went?

In some sense, that is one of the central questions of art. It is the question of how specific characters or scenes in literature, painting, sculpture, film, and so on can contribute to our lives. I will leave that question to the side, since to answer it would require a survey of the entire history of the philosophy of art. A more manageable question is this one: how might Lonergan's investigations of the characters' experience in these three films bring us a deeper understanding of the relation of death to suffering? Or, more pointedly, how might the experience of those characters bring us a deeper understanding of the suffering death causes that does not make us stronger, that cannot be redeemed for greater flourishing, that creates scars whose healing—if indeed there is healing—does not make us more whole? If we use the term "understanding" in a broad sense, to mean not only cognitive understanding but emotional understanding as well, we can begin to see our way to the outlines of an answer. That answer, however, can only be filled in through a reflection on the particular experiences themselves.

There are at least three types of understanding that may be gained through such a reflection. One is an understanding of the falsity of Nietzsche's aphorism; we recognize that what doesn't kill me often does not make me stronger. Of course we might say that we do not need recourse to art to convince us of this. And cognitively, this may be true. But emotionally, Lonergan's films bring us to an appreciation of this fact for which intellectual comprehension alone cannot be a substitute. It is one thing to *say* that I am not always made stronger by what fails to kill me. It is quite another to witness the ongoing torment of a man who has caused the death of his children, particularly after witnessing the love he has displayed toward them.[3]

Second, there is an understanding of different *ways* in which what doesn't kill one does not make one stronger. Here is where the particularity of the experiences becomes important. We move from a general understanding of the falsity of Nietzsche's aphorism to a more particular grasp of how deep suffering creates different wounds, depending on the kind of suffering that is inflicted, the kind of people it is inflicted upon, and the situations in which they find themselves. This is why a single movie will not really suffice for an adequate response to Nietzsche's aphorism. Philosophically, one can argue that a single counterexample would establish the aphorism's falsity. However, that would only be a narrow insight. What Lonergan's films offer us is a recognition of the wider range of scars created through suffering that cannot be redeemed for greater strength.[4]

Third, that wider range begins to show us something else, something that will be investigated on the plane of morality in the fourth chapter: the complexity of human beings. The opening line of Tolstoy's *Anna Karenina* reads, "All happy families resemble one another, but each unhappy family is unhappy in its own way." It's not clear that even *Anna Karenina* itself sustains the truth of the first half of that line, but it is certainly convincing on the latter half. Lonergan's films, one might say, show us much the same thing in relation to the suffering that death brings, both to families and to individuals. And in showing us that, he opens a window on to human complexity that would undermine any attempt to see our species as reducible to simple explanations, first in relation to suffering and later, as we will see, in relation to morality. As Lonergan himself says in the conversational voice-over to *Manchester by the Sea*, "You never meet a human being who is not a full human being in your life." (He says in reference to a discussion of the minor characters in *Manchester*, adding, "And I aspire to make that the case in the film.")

To see the particularity, and with it the complexity, of the wounds of suffering I will treat each film in turn. This chapter proceeds chronologically through the films, although the reason for this has nothing to do with the fact of chronology. Rather, it is the increasing difficulty of the relation to death that I'm interested in here. In *You Can Count on Me* (hereafter *Count*) the death is that of the parents, given at the outset of the film. It is a death with which their children, Samantha (often just "Sammy") and Terry, have to deal. In *Margaret*, the death is partially, although accidentally, caused by Lisa Cohen and the bus driver, Gerald Maretti, with whom she is conversing. Finally, in *Manchester by the Sea* (hereafter *Manchester*), Lee Chandler, through a bit of negligence, is the entire cause of his children's death.

Parental Death

Count opens with the Prescott parents driving home at night from some event they had attended. The scene is a pedestrian one. The audience faces the parents from outside the windshield of the car. The parents seem tired; it must be late. The first line of the film is the wife asking the husband, "Why do they always put braces on teenage girls at the exact moment they're most self-conscious about their appearance?" The husband replies, "I don't know," and then swerves to pass a car that has cut him off on the road. Out of the darkness a semi appears in the lane he has swerved into. The camera pans back to the couple, now in panic, as they see the semi hurtling toward them, and then closes. The next scene is of a police officer at the door of the Prescott home about to tell Sammy what has happened. (With typical Lonergan economy, we do not see the officer actually telling her about her parents' death, only the halting gesture on his face before he does so.)

Although the parents do not appear again in the film, except through flashbacks, and although we learn almost nothing more of them, the mother's words display the caring she has for her daughter, whose preadolescent face appears immediately after the accident when she answers the door to the police officer. The parents are clearly weary from their evening, and yet the mother is thinking about her daughter on the way home. When later, as grown-ups, Terry and Sammy are in the middle of an argument at a restaurant and she says, "I wish Mom was here" (and Terry agrees), we are not surprised to hear this. The only evidence we have of what kind of parents they were is given to us in the opening scene.

After the funeral, *Count* turns its attention to Sammy and Terry as adults. Sammy is a single parent of an 8-year-old boy, Rudy. (Lonergan comments in the conversational voice-over that Terry was 8 when his parents were killed. This is significant, since Terry forms a close bond with Rudy, suggesting that he has not matured much since his parents' death.) She works in a local bank in the small town of Scottsville in which they grew up, raises Rudy, and occasionally dates a local man, Bob, with whom she has had an on-and-off relationship. She is religious, confiding in a local pastor (played by Lonergan himself), and periodically suggesting to Terry that his problems stem in part from his distance from the church. She tries very hard to get along with everyone and to make sure everyone around her is okay. Laura Linney plays her character with a particular smile, one that appears at moments of potential tension in a relationship. The smile is both an offer and a plea for the other person to acknowledge that everything is okay, nothing a problem.

This desire for everything to be okay is reinforced periodically throughout the film. Sammy has an affair with her boss Brian, but decides to break it off, using words that she will also use when she earlier refused Bob's offer of marriage. In both cases she wants to make sure that, although she is breaking things off, they are "still friends." In contrasting Sammy and Terry, Lonergan comments that Sammy's problems are so buried inside her and Terry's so out in the open that it's easier for her to deal with his problems than with hers. Sammy seeks to cover everything over with a superficial veneer of mutual acceptance so that her pain cannot become manifest, even to her.

For someone like Sammy, Terry could not be more maddening. In some ways Terry has not matured a moment since his parents' death. Although he does not openly pine for them, he is emotionally still a child. Lonergan uses his friendship with Rudy to illustrate this. Early in their relationship Terry walks into Rudy's room at night and wakes him up. He tells Rudy that this used to be his room and advises Rudy to leave the town of Scottsville when he grows up to avoid being stuck there like his mother. During this scene Rudy is lying in bed while Terry is sitting cross-legged on the floor. The room is dark, illuminated only by the hall light outside. This could be two young friends talking during a sleepover. Later, when Terry is angry with Sammy for inviting the local pastor over for a talk with him, he reneges on an offer to take Rudy fishing in a display of petulance that is embarrassing to watch. Once, when he is babysitting Rudy while Sammy is out on a date with Bob, he takes him to a pool hall and then insists that Rudy lie to his mother about it.

In addition to his immaturity, Terry is a drifter. He has worked in Alaska, been jailed for a fight in Florida, and generally been unable to create a stable life for himself. In fact, he comes to town to visit Sammy for the purpose of borrowing money, since he's broke. However, although he is often juvenile and a drifter, he does not come off like a complete loser. There is something charming about him, something spontaneous that is fetching. This spontaneity contrasts with the closed-off way Sammy approaches the world. Instead of everything being in control and okay, Terry opens himself to experiences and does not feel the need to tamp down his life's energies. What he tells Rudy at night about their town may be ill-advised, but it isn't false. As Lonergan describes him in the voice-over, he isn't a thoughtless screwup, he's a thoughtful screwup.

Before turning to Terry and Sammy's relationship to each other and to their parents' death, it would be worth bearing in mind the central role of that death in *Count*. It is a shadow that is always there. Not only does the film open with the horrific scene of the crash, clearly the most violent scene in the movie even though the crash itself is not shown, there are reminders of the absence of the parents throughout. When Terry returns to Scottsville for the visit with his sister the bus passes by his parents' graveyard; he looks out and then looks back, clearly upset. Moreover, the film is nearly, but not quite, bookended with two scenes at the graveyard. In the first scene, Sammy lays flowers on their parents' graves, located in a graveyard that sits atop a pacific hillside. Then she kneels in front of one of the graves and prays. In the second scene we see Terry, who is about to leave town, sitting with his back resting against one of the graves looking out at the same pacific scene shown earlier. The parallelism in the ways the two scenes are shot is unmistakable (as is the contrast between the quiet beauty of the scene and the emotional turmoil throughout the film). The parents' absence is with sister and brother throughout, as is the contrast of their personalities brought out by their different behaviors at the gravesite. Sammy brings flowers and assumes an attitude of religious reverence, while Terry flouts gravesite protocol by propping himself up against a gravestone—a gesture that can remind us that the parents he wants to support him no longer can.

The parents' death is the constant background against which Sammy and Terry's lives and relationship play out. Sammy wants everything to stay under control. Everything must be okay. Her job, her relationships, the way she moves through the world: all of this must keep at bay any loose emotional ends that might escape her grasp. And yet there is one element of her world to which she is deeply attached that will disturb that world: Terry. When Sammy receives a letter from Terry near the beginning of the film announcing his visit, she is overjoyed. Her smile, which through much of *Count* is forced and accompanied by a look that asks for complicity, spreads across her face without constraint. Her relationship with her brother does not allow her to foresee the chaos he is about to bring into her world. (We will return to this point in the following chapter on self-deception.) Terry is the contradiction in her life, a contradiction that shows more clearly her project of control and that project's ultimate failure.

Perhaps there is nowhere in the film where this emerges more clearly than in the lunch they share at a restaurant right after Terry has returned. It is a difficult scene to watch. We have witnessed Sammy's elation at the announcement of Terry's visit. She takes him to a fancy restaurant—one imagines it as perhaps the only fancy restaurant in town—and wears a nice dress, a fact that Terry notices. This is a central scene in *Count*, one that Lonergan notes is the film's longest. What will emerge is that while for Sammy the visit is an opportunity to see the brother who has gone missing from her life for too long, for Terry the primary motive is to borrow money. Before that becomes clear, however, Terry reveals to Sammy that the reason he has been out of contact with her is that he has spent time in jail for participating in a bar fight.

This is the first confrontation we see between the control Sammy seeks and the chaos Terry brings. The idea that her brother has been in jail is too much for her. When Terry reveals this, she shouts "What?!" and the camera pans back to show everyone in the restaurant having stopped their conversations to look over at the table the two are sitting at. A crack has appeared in Sammy's project of making sure everything is okay, and the anxiety that emerges is underlined through its display to others in the restaurant. One can imagine here as well that her anxiety (manifested as anger) has not only to do with the fact of Terry's jail time as with a feeling of responsibility she might have as the older sister, the one who, in the absence of parents, is supposed to be a role model for her brother.

Terry, then, is the chaos Sammy cannot control. His life is characterized by drifting and failure. We are not told why this is; however, the suggestion is clear, just as it is for Sammy. *Count* jumps from the funeral for the parents near the beginning of the film to the present day, implying that what we are about to see results from what we have just seen. In Terry's case it is someone whose life has been at sea for many years, first drifting away from Scottsville, then as far as Alaska, and then as far from there as Florida. His first appearance in the film is as he is packing up to leave for Scottsville to ask Sammy for money. In his small and nearly unfurnished apartment is his girlfriend, a woman clearly much younger than he (again demonstrating his emotional immaturity). She is seeking displays of affection from him that he cannot or will not offer her; it is hard to imagine, as the film goes on, that he can offer closeness to much of anyone except, as we come to see, his sister and her child. While for Sammy the death of the parents has led to a project of building borders around her life as well as her emotions, for Terry it has led to the abandonment of committed projects altogether. For Sammy, nothing must escape her emotional management, while for Terry nothing can be managed. They are both projects that are ultimately bound to failure.

The failure of Terry's project is manifest. He has been unable to cobble together a coherent life. In many ways he has remained at the emotional level he had reached at the moment of his parents' death—this is one of the lessons of his friendship with Rudy. Eight-year-olds can be charming and are often spontaneous, but they are not yet prepared to undertake the long-term commitments that constitute most adult lives. In fact, they are not even prepared to commit to spontaneity as a life venture. Of course, Terry is not entirely an 8-year-old. He has had years of experience; Lonergan says he thinks of him as about 25 or 26 years old. He can talk about different parts of the country in contrast to his native Scottsville—which Sammy cannot. He can take Rudy fishing, drive a car, and play a mean game of pool. He can also do something else, something that Rudy, at his age, cannot do. He can undermine, at least for moments, Sammy's own project of control.

So far the focus has been on how Terry brings upset into Sammy's world. The great disappointment for her soon after he arrives is her realization that the primary motive for his visit is to borrow money. After she pulls money out of a banking machine for him she tells him, "I've been looking forward to seeing you more than anything! I've been telling everyone I know that you were coming home! I cleaned the whole fucking house so it would look nice for you! I thought you were gonna stay for at least a few days! It didn't occur to me that you were just broke again. I wish you would have just sent me an invoice!" But after this nadir a subtler change takes place in Sammy, one that seems to come from Terry's presence, although Lonergan does not make the connection too obvious. (He never makes anything too obvious.)

While at Sammy's house, Terry learns that his girlfriend had tried to commit suicide, and that her parents do not want him to have contact with her. He asks Sammy if he can stay at her house for a few days. While he is there Sammy begins to engage in behavior that one might have thought her incapable of before his arrival. Most pointedly, she has an affair with her boss, Brian, himself a controlling sort who rubs the employees of the bank the wrong way with nitpicking directives and a seeming inability to understand that he is operating in a small town rather than a large city. There is tension between Brian and Sammy from the outset, when Brian prohibits her from her previous practice of stepping out of the office for a few minutes each day to pick up Rudy from school. Over time, however, it becomes evident that he is unhappy in his marriage, and a dinner between them leads to sex and eventually a short affair.

One might wonder whether the tension between Sammy and Brian had a sexual tone from the outset that, even in Terry's absence, would eventually have developed into an affair. However, this is belied by the contrasting relationship Sammy is already in with the townsperson Bob. Although there are tensions in that relationship—Bob had been reluctant earlier to commit to Sammy and now she is reluctant in the face of his desire to commit—the relationship is portrayed as warm and supportive but not very passionate. This contrast suggests that it is Terry's presence that leads Sammy to transgress boundaries and invite some chaos into her life, a chaos that she clearly enjoys, as a conversation she has with Terry on the porch of her house later at night after the first sexual encounter with Brian reveals. When she confesses the affair, she does so with an abandon, an excitement, and a sense of naughtiness that we do not see elsewhere in her demeanor.

Lonergan comments in the voice-over that he had planned for Terry to have a liberating influence on Sammy but not for Sammy to have a domesticating influence on him. This is certainly the case in *Count*. But there is more. If Terry momentarily liberates Sammy, it is from a project that she formed in response to her parents' death, a project whose liberation also reveals its failure, and on two levels. First, and most obvious, the project is a failure because it cannot be carried through. From her angry outburst at lunch to her affair with her boss, Sammy cannot always make everything okay. She cannot tamp down her life into a settled order. It may have taken Terry's visit to reveal this, but it is in the end revealed. Second, on a subtler level, the project is a failure on its own terms. It is an unsatisfying way for her to live. When she transgresses the boundary of the boss/employee relationship with Brian, she experiences a thrill of the kind we cannot imagine her to have had for many years. If Terry's presence elicits that in her, it also displays the emotionally unsatisfying life she has been leading up until then.

We do not know the entire trajectory of Sammy's and Terry's life that led them to the point where Sammy is concerned with containment and Terry with chaos. It is precisely because we do not know this, because the film leaps from the parents' funeral to the present, that we are meant to see the connection between the death and the current state of their lives. And it is not hard to imagine how it could have been like this. How does a child survive the death of his or her parents? Moreover, Scottsville is a small town; when Terry denigrates it to Rudy in their discussion late at night one does not feel that he is wrong. In Scottsville, Sammy and Terry will always be identified with their parents' death. The continuity of the events is subtly underlined for us when Terry arrives for his visit. The first person to talk with him when he walks through the downtown after stepping off the bus is the police officer who, years earlier, had come to the Prescott's door to inform Sammy of the death of their parents. How does one deal with that as they grow up?

One way is to try to ensure that the devastation does not visit one again, to make sure that everything is always okay. Things must be kept under control so that the pain that is everywhere on the horizon of one's life and from one's town cannot find its way in. It is a way of coping that fits well into a town like Scottsville. Everything there is ordered, since everyone knows everyone else's business. All one has to do is slip into that order and participate in maintaining it. Of course one has more significant stakes than the other townspeople in doing this. And it can leave one emotionally bereft. However, it is at least a way of coping that on the surface makes sense. Moreover, for women, who are supposed to fit in rather than make waves, it is an option that might be warmly encouraged by the town's norms.

Another way is to rebel against the town itself and all its associations with one's parents' death. It is to refuse to come to terms with the desolation that death has caused. Instead, one runs away and, since the death will always have been there, one keeps running. It is perhaps easier to imagine a male doing this than a female, given traditional gender roles. However, it is the very fact of running that keeps death close at hand. We are given a glimpse of this early in *Count* when Terry is on the bus coming into Scottsville. He rides past a graveyard, which we have already seen earlier from another angle when Sammy was placing flowers at their parents' grave. He looks out at the graveyard and then turns away with a pained expression. Their death has not left him; rather, in important ways it has defined him, run away from it as he might.

The death of Sammy and Terry's parents did not kill them, but neither did it make them stronger. It left them with wounds that have only very partially healed. This is obvious in Terry's case. He is, as Lonergan tells us, a thoughtful screwup. In Sammy's case the wounding is more subtle, since she has figured out how to carry on in Scottsville. But it comes out in her gestures, for instance in the smile that seeks to make everything okay and the outbursts that come when the order of her world gets upset. This is not to say that either of them is reducible to their wounds. There is more to them than this, a more that emerges in their relationship. Terry, through his very immaturity, offers Sammy a glimpse into emotional abandon that she takes up in her affair. Sammy, for her part, offers Terry a love that he cannot find, or at least cannot accept, anywhere else. In addition, her world offers him Rudy, someone who brings him out of himself even though—or perhaps precisely because—he cannot relate to him as an adult relates to a child. "You never meet a human being who is not a full human being." Sammy and Terry help bring out the full humanity in each other—to the extent that it can be brought out, given the depth of their wounds.

And that, precisely, is the point. They are not killed by their wounds, but neither do those wounds entirely heal. Because of this they are not made stronger. They both survive in their different ways, bearing the scars of their parents' death, neither entirely succumbing to them nor molding them into something greater. And isn't that true for the rest of us, even those who have not lost parents during childhood? Many of our griefs, perhaps most of them, although they don't kill us, do not make us stronger. We survive most of the bereavements of our lives, the losses that are carved into us, not through an overcoming, but instead through soldiering on as best we can, if we're lucky with the support of those we love, those we can count on.

Causing Death

The plot of *Margaret* takes place against the background of a larger canvas than does *Count*. First, the canvas is literally larger: New York City as opposed to Scottsville. Moreover, the larger background of the city plays a more overtly prominent role in *Margaret* than the small town did in the earlier film. In *Count*, there is much that is implied about the role of the town in forming and framing the main characters' lives. However, in *Margaret* the city is never far from the viewers' awareness. The film opens with a slow-motion scene of people walking along the crowded streets of what looks like midtown New York as the opening credits roll. Scenes like this reappear periodically throughout the film, and they are the only ones in slow motion. The effect it has—at least on this viewer—is one of emphasizing how many different lives are unfolding in the city. It's as though the drama we are about to witness (or, as the film unfolds, are witnessing) is one drama among the many that are happening in this city at this moment. Of course the film itself, with its many dramas, also shows us this. But the role of the scenes of slow-motion walkers, as well as periodic shots panning across city buildings or upon the traffic from the height of one of those buildings or, in an interesting cinematic move, occasionally focusing on the conversations of strangers who are (and sometimes are not) in the frame when the main characters are in view, is to never let us forget the fact that the death that Lisa Cohen and those around her are dealing with is a brushstroke on a very large canvas. (The occasional long pans of the sky over Manhattan also remind us that the film, although released in 2011, was created in 2005, after the events of 9/11.)

Before turning to that brushstroke, let me introduce a personal note that may affect my viewing of those scenes of the city. I grew up in New York, and in fact, from what I can tell perhaps just a few blocks from where Monica Patterson is hit and killed by the bus Gerald Maretti is driving. I would often gaze out the window of my bedroom, or the living room of a friend, or a restaurant window, and watch the people walking or talking on the street or even the windows of apartments whose people I could not see, and wonder what their lives were like. In small towns, it seems to me, having lived in one for several decades, easier to think of one's own life and those immediate lives around one as all the lives there are. In a large city, particularly one like New York where people are pressed together, that is a much more difficult illusion to maintain. Lonergan's interspersing of these city scenes in the film brought me back to those moments in my own life and, I believe, offers them more generally to the viewers, fostering the recognition that one's own life is only one among many that are taking place at that very moment.

Having said that, however, there is another way in which the city plays less of a role in the lives of *Margaret*'s characters than Scottsville does in the lives of Sammy and Terry. Although New York City *frames* Lisa's life and the lives of those around her, it does not contribute in the same way toward *structuring* it. Sammy and Terry are constrained by the small town in which they live; they must either accommodate themselves to it or reject it. *Count* shows us, through these siblings, both options. The drama that occurs in *Margaret* did not need New York City in order to happen. It could have happened in any large city, or perhaps even in a smaller one. To be sure, the characters in the film, particularly those like Emily—to whom we will return—do seem like products of New York. But the events themselves and the way those events affect the film's characters do not require anything more than a general urban background. In this sense, the many scenes we are shown of walking, of buildings, and even of the sky assume a role relative to the audience more than to the film's characters or its drama.

Let us turn now to that drama. Lisa Cohen (Anna Paquin), a young woman in full adolescent hormonal overdrive, is a student at an elite Manhattan private school. She is shown in class, among peers, flirting with her teacher, losing her virginity, fighting with her brother, alternately relying on and screaming at (and being screamed at by) her mother. The heart of the plot, however, begins when she is trying to buy a cowboy hat for a horseback riding trip her father (who is divorced from her mother and living in Santa Monica) has offered to take her on. Her attention is caught by a cowboy hat being worn by a bus driver, Gerald Maretti (Mark Ruffalo). Although she does not make it on to the bus to ask him about the hat before the doors close, she runs alongside the bus trying to signal him that she's interested in where he got the hat. Maretti, clearly enjoying the playful back-and-forth, loses his concentration on the street, runs a red light, and hits a woman, Monica Patterson (Allison Janney), whose agonized death throes are presented in their full unfolding while Lisa tries to comfort her. As she dies, she asks for her daughter, also named Lisa.

The police arrive, and Lisa and Maretti are questioned independently. We do not hear Maretti's answers, but see him looking at Lisa during his questioning. She is asked whether she noticed that the light was red or green and, after some hesitation, says she guesses it was green.

There are a number of plot lines that follow in *Margaret*, which, as mentioned, is over three hours in the extended cut. For the moment our interest is in how Lisa (with a nod to Emily and Maretti) copes with the death. Lisa and Maretti are directly involved in the death itself. They caused it not through intent but accidentally. In this causing, Maretti is more at fault, of course, because he is responsible as the bus driver. There is little to lay at Lisa's doorstep except that she should not have been distracting the bus driver. However, and unsurprising, because she was part of the causal chain leading to the death, she is confronted with a guilt that structures much of her reaction to it. Moreover, later she decides—or perhaps admits—that the bus driver ran the light and that she lied to cover for Maretti's negligence. (The film cuts rapidly back-and-forth at that moment among several points of view—Lisa's, the bus driver's, and Monica Patterson's—but seems to show from Lisa's point of view the light turning red.)

How might one cope with a death one has helped cause? There can be many reactions, and even a tacking back-and-forth among them. Lisa, because she is an adolescent going through swift mood changes, displays a number of them openly: guilt, denial, the attempt to shift blame, turning her attention to something else. But these reactions, and sometimes more than one at the same time, are characteristic of many of us who cause, however inadvertently, harm to another. The shadow of the death is an undercurrent haunting Lisa throughout the film. However, if we are to portray a life in its fullness, we should recognize that in most cases this haunting is embedded in a number of other life events, a trajectory that includes such activities as going about one's daily tasks, interacting with others who have only an indirect or even no relation to the harm one has participated in causing, and generally moving physically through a world that existed before one caused harm and continues to exist after one has caused it. (In the case where one causes the death of one's own children, though, this trajectory might become wrapped around that single event, as we will see.)

However, as Lonergan's film insists, these general themes appear only in particular ways in particular lives, and to understand them we need to see them in their embeddedness in those lives. *Margaret*, because it is a film painted on a wide canvas, offers us this embeddedness with a fullness that a shorter film would not be able to accomplish. Since we cannot adequately summarize that fullness—after all, that's what the film is for—let's focus instead on several moments of Lisa's haunting: her relationship with Emily, her very brief direct relationship with Maretti, and her relationship (inseparable from the first two) to the legal process of getting compensation for some of Monica Patterson's distant family members for the accident.

After Monica's death, Lisa seeks to contact her family members for reasons that are unclear, probably even to Lisa. Eventually she runs across one of Monica's closest friends, Emily. She attends a small wake that Emily has organized and becomes closer to Emily as the film progresses. Through Emily, Lisa seems to be trying to develop a relationship with Monica and, relatedly, to come to terms with this traumatic death in which she has had a part, however inadvertent. At one point Lisa angers Emily by telling her that she felt as though, as Monica was dying, she actually played the part of her daughter in her last moments. The daughter, however, had died of leukemia when she was young, a fact which Lisa was already aware of. Emily responds, "this isn't an opera! And we are not all supporting characters to the drama of your amazing life!" (The themes of opera and drama are leitmotifs of the film. Lisa's mother, Joan [J. Smith-Cameron, Lonergan's real-life spouse], is an actress in a play significantly entitled *Controversy*; operatic music often plays in the film's slow-motion scenes; and the film ends with Lisa and Joan attending an opera.)

This response is cutting, in part because it is true. Lisa, after all, is an adolescent and, like a lot of adolescents, acts in an overly dramatized self-centered way. But in another way the response is unfair. Lisa is trying to come to terms with an event that is larger than her ability to cope with, indeed larger than many people's ability to cope with. She has been the partial cause of someone's death, and she wants to come to terms with that. Feeling as though she might have offered some comfort to the dying woman might help in that project, as does her vicarious relationship with Monica through Monica's friend Emily. One of the things we come to understand through this relationship is precisely that there is no real coming to terms with one's participation in this death. It eludes any attempt at psychological reconciliation.

In this sense, Lisa's relation to the death contrasts with that of Emily's. Although Emily and Lisa both seek to hold Maretti responsible for the death—a point we will return to—Emily's relationship to the death of her friend is "cleaner," less vexed. She grieves the loss of her friend and wants to hold the bus driver responsible, but she is not subject to any extra turmoil that cannot be managed.

Lisa's relationship to the bus driver Maretti is, understandably, more complicated. Maretti, although a central figure in the film's plot, only appears three times, and the last time only very briefly. His first appearance is during the crash scene. His final appearance is near the end of the film when Lisa sees him driving a bus at night while waiting to go to the opera with her mother. The only other time we see Maretti is when Lisa goes to his house in an attempt to talk with him about the death. As with Emily, it is unclear to us and probably to Lisa why she is doing this. She is seeking some sort of reconciliation with the death, and Maretti is probably the last person from whom she would likely get it. Her interaction with him does not go well. His wife is clearly wondering whether there is an affair involved, and Maretti himself insists on the story they both told the police—that the light was green. Lisa, meanwhile, is trying to convince him that they had a tacit understanding that they would lie to the police. She recalls, correctly, that he was looking over at her when he gave his rendering of the events right after the crash, and she insists that this was because they had an unspoken agreement about what to say. Maretti knows the stakes of all this for him and asks her whether she wants him to lose his job and challenges her to say who would take care of his family if he goes to jail. Moreover, he insists, the woman is dead and there isn't anything anyone can do about that. In the end he refuses to engage with her any further, leading to her full determination to hold him responsible for the death.

While Lisa's relationships with both Emily and Maretti are both failed projects to come to terms with the death, they are complicated ones, characterized by ambivalence and uncertainty. Her relationship to the project of holding Maretti responsible, a project she engages in with Emily, is more straightforward. We might put it this way: if she can have Maretti held responsible, that means he was the one who killed Monica Patterson, not her—or at least not *only* her. Lisa pursues this project with abandon, meeting with a series of lawyers and insisting that monetary damages are not enough—Maretti must be fired. There is a complication, however. The nearest surviving relatives—those who would receive monetary damages—are a cousin in Arizona, Abigail Berlitz, and her husband. Abigail, whom Emily does not hold in high esteem, is clear that she's interested in the money and doesn't care what happens to the bus driver. When, in the negotiations, their attorney says that the city will settle for $350,000 but will not discipline or fire Maretti for political reasons, Abigail and her husband take the offer. Lisa's reaction is one of the more poignant and revealing moments in the film. She leaps out of her chair and shouts, "I'm the one who killed her! I'm the one who killed her! But at least I know I did it, and that guy has no idea! And he's wandering around blaming everybody else and all I want is for somebody to let him know that what he did was wrong!" before stalking out of the room.

It is at that moment that Lisa's ongoing suffering for participating, however unwittingly, in Monica Patterson's death is revealed openly. Over the course of the film the audience has become used to Lisa's outbursts: at her brother, at her mother, at classmates (although never at her distant father, who probably most deserves them—a story for the following chapter). But this moment in the film feels different. It is not adolescent hormonal rage that Lisa expresses, but instead an aloneness with a death she cannot come to terms with: not through contact with Monica's family and friends, not though a vicarious identification with her daughter, and not through either collusion with or shifting the blame to Maretti. A tragedy has occurred, a tragedy that she can neither undo nor come to terms with, and it is a tragedy partly of her making. Although she is not broken by this—we see, throughout *Margaret*, various other aspects of her life that show that she cannot be said to succumb to it—neither does it make her stronger. While Maretti cannot, for the little we see of him, let his participation in the death into full consciousness, and while Emily, in contrast to both Lisa and Maretti, has no reminder of the kind that would haunt her, Lisa can neither suppress nor accommodate the death she has helped cause. *Margaret* closes with Lisa and her mother weeping in each other's arms at an opera they are attending. (It is also a typical ending moment for Lonergan's films: a reconciliation that is at once touching and painful, and pregnant with a future that offers no guarantees.)

I want to suggest here that the poem after which the film is named suggests that Lisa is not alone in carrying around such feelings. Very few of us will participate in the death of another. And yet we carry our moments of regret, moments that we can neither abandon nor integrate into our lives. And there will be other moments as well, moments that perhaps we do not participate in, tragedies we had no part in causing, but that nevertheless haunt us; we carry them like scars in our lives that will not heal.

> ás the heart grows older
> It will come to such sights colder
> By and by, nor spare a sigh
> Though worlds of wanwood leafmeal lie;
> And yet you will weep and know why...

It is the blight man was born for,
It is Margaret you mourn for.

Over the course of *Margaret*, Lisa has grown. The insight she expresses at the attorney's office reveals that growth. It is not, however, a growth that makes her more whole, that brings her to a place of peace or settled maturity or greater uprightness. Rather, it is a growth into one of the fractures that open up in all lives and that opened up, because of its circumstances, with particular force in hers. If, as Lonergan tells us, you never meet a human being who is not a full human being, at the same time you never meet one who is entirely whole, one without wounds or whose wounds have all healed. At the end of *Margaret*, we know that Lisa will not be broken by what has happened and what she has done. However, we also know that it will never entirely leave her either, and that it will likely not make her stronger.

The early death of one's parents and the death one has participated in of strangers are calamities that can resist integration. Even so, one can conceive and carry on a life after them, if not entirely beyond them. What happens when a moment is so catastrophic that one cannot get beyond it, cannot envision a future for oneself, cannot loosen the grip it has on one's life? What happens when the tragedy wraps itself around a life, becoming not a wound or a scar but the very definition of one's existence?

Causing the Death of One's Children

When *Manchester by the Sea* opens, Lee Chandler (Casey Affleck) is with his brother and nephew on a boat. The nephew is young, perhaps

10 or 12. They are fishing. Lee is kidding with his nephew Patrick (played as a young child by Ben O'Brien) about how sharks like to eat kids. The nephew is arguing back and they are both laughing. It is unclear at this moment whether the kid is Lee's nephew or his son. There is clearly a warm affection between them.

A few minutes into the film the scene switches and we see Lee, now a handyman for an apartment building, shoveling snow alone and then fixing the plumbing of residents there. (In the voice-over, Lonergan tells us this is about five years after the scene on the boat.) He is morose, eyes often downcast, with a resigned air that contrasts with the scene the audience has just witnessed. He gets into an argument with a woman who is acting snottily toward him while he's looking for a leak in her shower, and when she asks him whether he thinks she should take a shower in front of him just so he can find where her shower leaks, he replies, "I don't really give a fuck what you do, Mrs. Olsen. I just want to find the leak," prompting her to kick him out of her apartment. Later, after his boss berates him for this, we see him at a bar, where a woman tries to flirt with him only to find him nearly unresponsive—not unfriendly, but unsocial to the point of awkwardness. He becomes increasingly drunk and winds up picking a fight with two men across the bar who are talking and occasionally cast glances at him.

The audience does not know what has happened to Lee Chandler, only that he is very much unlike the person at the outset of the film, and Lonergan is in no hurry to let us know why this is. We don't find out until nearly an hour into the film that on a drunken night between the scene on the boat and his becoming a handyman Lee went to the store for some groceries, seemingly forgetting to put the screen back on the fireplace after he had put some logs in it, and one of the logs must have rolled out and started a fire that burned the house down and killed his three young children. Significantly—for reasons we will see in the following chapter—we learn this from Lee himself, who reconstructs what must have happened during a police interview the morning following the fire. In recounting the events, Lee explains that the reason he was using logs instead of central heating was that the latter dries out his wife Randy's (Michelle Williams) sinuses. His tragic mistake is motivated by the care he has for his wife.

It should be noted here that this explanation, offered with a deadened but clearly shell-shocked emotion, calls to mind the countenance we have seen and will continue to see of Lee Chandler as the film progresses. There is his life before the fire and after the fire, or perhaps better, before the fire and the fire itself—since the fire is always immediately present to him. (The fire scene, one of the more harrowing scenes in recent cinema, is shown right before the interview just mentioned. It is shown with Pachelbel's *Canon* playing and no other sounds except his wife Randy's screaming for her kids as she is being removed from the area of the fire.)

The fire is the pivot around which the film revolves. On the one side, in between the bar fight and the fire scene, the plot of the film is set up, along with flashbacks that remind the audience of Lee's previous happy life with his family. Lee's brother Joe (Kyle Chandler) has died from a heart condition that we have already learned would be fatal to him and, unbeknownst to Lee, has appointed Lee as (the now high school student) Patrick's (Lucas Hedges) guardian. Patrick's mother is out of the picture, having earlier been witnessed lying on a couch half-naked in an alcoholic slumber. On the far side of the fire scene is Lee's unfolding relationship with Patrick and the town of Manchester, which he left soon after the fire and, for all we know, has never been to again until the death of his brother. We will return to these relationships in this and the following chapter.

We should linger a moment, however, over what has happened to Lee. He is shown in flashbacks to be deeply attached to his children, as well as to his brother and nephew. He is a working-class man from what seems like a working-class town on the coast outside of Boston, a town where people are neither wealthy nor impoverished and where everyone knows everyone else's business. We imagine Lee's life before the fire as a fortunate one, not without conflict (earlier on the night of the fire his wife is angry with him and his friends for making so much noise in Lee's basement), but essentially happy. The contrast with his life after the fire could hardly be starker.

How does one, we might ask, ever get over causing the death of one's children, and moreover doing so through such a small mistake, through neglecting an act that, afterward, one must have sought to correct in one's mind a thousand times? (This possibility falls under the philosophical category of "moral luck."[5]) Consider the small things we trace back over in our minds to correct what we actually said or did: the outburst at a colleague we would take back, the homeless person we should not have passed on the street without giving money, the clever retort we thought of moments after that snide remark someone made. "If I could do it again …" "I should have said …" These possibilities haunt us for short periods, sometimes hobbling our ability to think of other things. And now imagine a mistake—a mistake that happens because we were drunk although we didn't need to be, we went to the store although there was nothing we urgently had to buy, we didn't listen to our spouse tell us to shut up and get to bed when we should have, we just didn't put the screen back on the fireplace—that results in the death of our children. It is not difficult to imagine the tape of other possibilities playing over and over in our heads until it crowds out most everything else, until it takes everything we have to focus on getting through the day. As Lonergan puts the point in the voice-over, "He's a guy who's trying to keep the walls from caving in every single day of his life."

We can contrast Lee Chandler's suffering with that of Sammy and Terry Prescott, but particularly that of Lisa Cohen. For Sammy and Terry, their lives are lived with scars that will never entirely heal. The closest they come to wholeness is in the moments in which they connect with each other, in which Terry's spontaneity draws Sammy out of her shell of control without his going so far as to evoke anger. A delicate balance, always fragile, and always revealing in its fragility the impossible projects each has embarked upon in response to their parents' deaths. However, although they underwent the deaths, they did not cause them. They had at least the innocence of being purely the victims of their parents' dying.

Lisa, however, did cause a death, or, more precisely, participated in causing a death. However, first, it was not the death of anyone she knew; it was the death of a stranger. In fact, her attempt to get closer to the life that was lost through her relationship with Emily displays that. She wanted to participate in a life—or at least see herself as a participant in a life—that would be forever barred from her, and that by her own action. To be sure, that action was inadvertent, and one might want to say that she shared that inadvertence with Lee Chandler's action (or inaction—a distinction without a difference here). And to that extent, shouldn't her reaction mirror his?

It isn't the same, though. This is the second point. Not only was her participation in the death indirect: she, after all, was not driving the bus. Moreover, her negligence was less egregious. It was not her job to ensure that the bus was driven safely. Yes, she should not have distracted the driver. But ultimately the responsibility for operating the bus safely is not hers. It could easily have been said that the most important contributant to Monica Patterson's death was Maretti's failure to hew to basic standards of bus driving practice. And this much, at least, is right in Lisa's and Emily's attempt to hold Maretti responsible for what happened—although, as we have seen, there is more to that attempt than simply an analytic attempt to ascribe responsibility.

Lee Chandler does not have that excuse. It was his responsibility to put the screen back in front of the fireplace. Put starkly, he did not contribute to his children's deaths—he caused them. He, and he alone. Lisa's attempt to hold Maretti responsible had an element of truth to it. In Lee's case, there was nowhere to turn except inside himself, which is precisely what he did. Granted, there was a good measure of misfortune in what happened. As he describes the likely unfolding events to the police, he suspects that a log rolled out of the fireplace and on to the floor. That doesn't always happen, and nothing he did directly caused it to happen. (In that sense, one might try to make the case that he has less responsibility than Maretti. After all, Maretti should have known that in a crowded city distracted bus driving would likely result in harm where Lee should not necessarily have suspected that a log would roll off the fire. But that is hardly comfort when it does.) And, in fact, in a moment we will return to in the next chapter, one of the fire marshals responds to Lee's incomprehension that after his confession he is not about to be arrested by saying, "You made a horrible mistake. Like a million other people did last night. But we don't wanna crucify you. It's not a crime to leave the screen off the fireplace."

But Lee knows, and cannot ever stop knowing, that there is a difference between his mistake and the mistake of those million other people. And he knows that the indirect element of the misfortune of the log rolling on to the floor cannot save him from responsibility for the death of his children. There is nowhere to turn except himself. He is responsible, and he can do nothing other than hollow himself out on a daily basis in response to that fact. He did try to escape once, grabbing the gun of one of the police officers when exiting the interview and trying to kill himself. But when he was prevented from that there was nothing left to do but soldier on with a knowledge he could neither accommodate nor elude.

This situation might bring us back to Nietzsche's aphorism, but from a different angle. What doesn't kill me makes me stronger. Maybe we should interpret Lee's causing the death of his children as having killed him. Of course it did not kill him in any literal sense. Although he tried to kill himself immediately after the event, he did not succeed and instead sought to live out his days just "trying to keep the walls from caving in." But Nietzsche's aphorism is not meant to be taken literally either. The aphorism does not intend for us to understand that it is only those things that do not end our lives that make us stronger, any more than it intends us to think that vitamins make us stronger because they don't kill us. It is the challenges that don't defeat us that are supposed to make us stronger.

Perhaps, then, we should consider the possibility that Lee's action metaphorically killed him. It defeated him so profoundly that he could not stitch together a meaningful life afterward. The structure of *Manchester* might lead us in this direction as well. Nearly the first half of the film unfolds before the fire and the rest after. This might seem a bit forced, since much of the action of the first half of the film takes place after the fire. However, what causes Lee to act as he does is not revealed until we see the fire. So should we take *Manchester* as a film in which Nietzsche's aphorism is, if not fulfilled, at least not denied?[6]

Things turn out to be more complicated than that. So far we have said very little about Lee's relationship with his nephew Patrick. The reason Lee returns to Manchester is because of the death of his brother, Joe. Patrick's mother is not, to Lee's knowledge, in the picture. (As it turns out Patrick has had surreptitious contact with his mother through e-mail and will later meet her and her new husband in an entirely awkward encounter.) As we have mentioned, when he returns he discovers that Joe's will has named him as Patrick's guardian, a role he clearly feels he cannot play. This causes conflict both within Lee and between him and Patrick. At first, Patrick insists that he does not need a guardian. Later, he accuses Lee of doing anything to get rid of his responsibility for him. On Lee's part, he eventually does make an attempt to move back to Manchester. We see him looking for jobs and getting denied at every turn. The denial, it is suggested, is motivated by the fact that he is *The* Lee Chandler, as several characters refer to him, the guy who killed his kids with his negligence. After he leaves the first place he looks for a job, the boss tells the worker who had talked with him, "I don't want to see him in here again."

The challenge of moving back to Manchester is underscored by something the audience has been exposed to before: the scene of the fire. The fire scene is not shown continuously but is alternated with shots of Lee sitting in the attorney's office learning that he is supposed to be Patrick's guardian. Seeing the juxtaposition reinforces the association in Lee's mind between being in Manchester and the fire. It is when the possibility of his having to move back to the town arises that the flashback to the fire occurs in the film. That association is the defining characteristic of the town for Lee, and so even to consider moving back there would require an enormous psychological counterweight. And there is one: Patrick.

Gradually over the second half of *Manchester* Lee develops an emotional connection (or perhaps better: reconnection) to Patrick that brings him outside himself just far enough to act for, what he hopes will be, Patrick's welfare. On the one hand, in the only sequence in which we see him smile in a way that reminds us of the old Lee Chandler, the one we saw at the outset of the movie, after denying that they can buy a new motor for Joe's boat, Lee decides to sell Joe's classic gun collection in order to pay for a new motor. (The smile appears when Lee is on the boat watching Patrick show his girlfriend how to drive it. It is clearly a reference to the beginning of the movie.) On the other hand, we should not be tempted to think of this relationship as Lee's emotional resurrection. The film makes this clear. Lee continues to have a profound inability or unwillingness to relate to others, exemplified by a strained social encounter with the mother of one of Patrick's girlfriends and later by another fight in a bar after a chance meeting with his ex-wife Randy—a scene to which we will return to in a moment.

Patrick's adolescent energy as well as his history with Lee helps Lee connect to him and brings him out of his shell ever so slightly. The importance of adolescence, it might be noted, is a recurring theme in

Lonergan's work. *Margaret* centers on the experience of an adolescent, Terry Prescott has adolescent tendencies, and if we look back to Lonergan's dramatic work, his first play, *This Is Our Youth*, it concerns people at the far end of their adolescence (ages 19–21). It is as though there is a certain openness to the world that adolescents display that can serve as a counterweight to the burdens that life eventually places on all of us. In any event, it has an effect on Lee, allowing him to re-form an emotional attachment to Patrick that is undoubtedly his first such emotional attachment since the fire.

So if the fire did not kill Lee, might we revisit Nietzsche's aphorism from another angle and say that it was indeed fulfilled? The fire did not kill him; so did it make him stronger? This, too, would be a mistake. Through his growing relationship with Patrick, we learn that the fire did not kill him. It damaged him in a way that he will never recover from, but it did not kill him. But neither did it make him stronger. It was something other than the fire, it was Patrick—or, more precisely, his relationship with Patrick—that made him (again, ever so slightly) stronger. What didn't kill him is not what made him stronger. Instead, it was something else.

And, as the audience learns, that something else turns out not to be enough to keep him in Manchester. A chance encounter with Randy convinces him of this. They meet on a street where Randy is strolling her newborn and talking with a friend of hers. The friend sees Lee and begs off, leaving the two of them alone. Randy wants to have lunch with Lee in order to be able to talk with him somehow. She apologizes for things she said to him after the fire. We don't know what she did say, but we can imagine it. She tells him now, "my heart was broken. It's always gonna be broken. I know your heart is broken too. But

I don't have to carry…I said things that I should—I should fuckin' burn in hell for what I said." (This is a revelation in the film. In earlier scenes in her new life she looks more put together than she had with Lee, and her pregnancy seemed to indicate that she had, much more than Lee, moved on with her life.) Lee tries to deflect this but then she says, "I love you. Maybe I shouldn't say that. And I'm sorry." All of this is too much for Lee. He tells her, "There's nothing there," and turns away. Lonergan, who admitted that he cried when he watched this scene filmed, comments in the voice-over, "Here you see how much they love each other and yet it's too late." It is too late, and it is also too much. The relationship with Patrick is sustainable, but to have any kind of relationship with Randy will bring him too close to the pain he can hardly keep at bay in any event.

And so he must leave Manchester, and Patrick. Over dinner Lee tells him, "I can't beat it. I'm sorry." Patrick starts to weep and, in a gesture Lee would have been incapable of at the beginning of the film, Lee gets out of his chair and hugs him. Arrangements are made for Lee and Joe's friend George (C. J. Wilson) to adopt Patrick until he comes of age, and, in a scene of characteristic ambiguity, we see Lee and Patrick walking away from Joe's funeral, bouncing a ball between them. Lee says that he will keep an extra room in his house for Patrick, another sign that there has been some emotional connection developed between them. But it remains unclear how much contact they will have, and how much that contact will contribute to any healing Lee may undergo, or even be capable of.

Lee's inadvertent act (or omission) causing his children's death did not kill him, although it nearly did. But neither did it make him stronger. It is, instead, because our lives are not reducible to a single act, as the death penalty opponent Bryan Stevenson often says, "Each of us is more than the worst thing we've ever done,"[7] there existed for Lee the possibility of not being entirely dead. Sometimes, although not killed, we are not made stronger by what doesn't kill us. Sometimes we are made stronger by something else entirely. We carry our wounds with us—and in Lee's case those wounds could not have cut more deeply—but perhaps, circumstances permitting, other aspects of our world come forth that, while they may not heal, permit some salve to be applied. Patrick does not make Lee whole; nothing will. But because he is who he is—and, in contrast to Randy, because he is not associated too deeply with the tragedy itself—he allows Lee to recover at least some shards of his previous emotional life.

Conclusion

As I noted at the outset, the falsity of Nietzsche's aphorism does not lie in its always being false. Nor does it lie in the opposite's always being true. It lies instead in the fact that there is no *always* to be had here. The investigation of different relations of different people to different deaths in Lonergan's films reveals this to us. A mistake often made in philosophy—we will return to this in the conclusion of this book—is to seek absolutes where there are only particulars, or at best generalizations that hold only more or less. While his aphorism may be inspiring—or alternatively, dispiriting to those who feel they cannot live up to it—an understanding of what happens to us when we are not killed by events requires knowing who we are and what circumstances we find ourselves in. Sammy and Terry Prescott display divergent ways of dealing with the death of their parents; Lisa Cohen and Gerald Maretti cope with a death they have participated in in entirely distinct ways, ways having to do not only with who they are but also with the situations they inhabit. For Lee Chandler, the act (or omission) he performed cannot do otherwise than define the trajectory of the rest of his life; the question is only how much that trajectory will be reducible to the moment of that act.

Through an investigation of characters who are, as Lonergan puts it, "full human beings," he has shown us that who we are and what we become in the face of tragedy resists easy accounting. It is, of course, easy to say this. In not just saying but rather showing us this, however, Lonergan offers the opportunity to come to more than a distant ratification of a general truth. More than this, he also allows us to understand not only ourselves but others as well, to experience the fullness of human beings whose sufferings cannot be evaded.

You Can Count on Me, *Margaret*, and *Manchester by the Sea* are often difficult to watch. This is because, among other things, we come to relate to these full human beings in trying, even tragic circumstances. We know that, like the rest of us, they will never entirely overcome those circumstances, but we hope they will not entirely succumb to them either. A heroic aphorism of the type that Nietzsche offers us cannot but conceal the complexity of all this, a complexity that is at once cognitive and emotional. Lonergan, by contrast, brings us back into the world where tragedy leads to suffering that is often something other than merely a challenge to be overcome. It is instead the source of scars that never entirely heal in lives that are never entirely whole. But, for reasons that are as complex as the scars themselves, those lives are never entirely destitute either.

3

Self-Deception

Where there is suffering, there is the temptation of self-deception. There can be many reasons for this. It might be that I don't want to admit the cause of my suffering because it would be embarrassing or depressing or because admitting it would bring back painful memories. Or it might be that I don't want to admit the very fact that I'm suffering: it would be a sign of weakness or insecurity. Or alternatively, it might be that I want to overemphasize the suffering itself, so I ascribe a depth to my wounds that, if I were honest with myself, I would have to admit don't exist.

The theme of self-deception is one that Lonergan himself recognizes as helping to structure his work. In his discussions with Rebecca Mead he says that part of his work is structured around the idea "that a large part of yourself is hidden from yourself, and comes out in all sorts of strange and interesting ways."[1] He ascribes his interest in this to his being raised by a mother and stepfather who were practicing psychoanalysts. And, as we saw in the introduction, he wrote the screenplay for *Analyze This*.

The fact is that we all deceive ourselves at various points in our lives. This self-deception can be about small things. We find ourselves watching a basketball game and then rooting for a team that is about to lose, so we tell ourselves that we really weren't that interested in the game after all. Or we offer a flimsy excuse to ourselves (and to others) for our child's misbehavior at school one day. Self-deception is an everyday phenomenon. Or we don't admit to ourselves that we're a bit relieved that our colleague didn't get that promotion that we didn't even apply for. However, it drives deeper when it concerns aspects of ourselves that we would rather not see, when self-awareness would reveal us to ourselves in a harsh or unflattering light. Moreover, the more we value ourselves as *not* being the way we would not like to see, the stronger the temptation to self-deception. This is particularly true in areas like morality. I often tell my students that while people's capacity for knowingly doing evil is quite limited, their capacity for self-deception seems nearly infinite.

The suffering that many of Lonergan's characters undergo often leads to various forms of self-deception—and in one important case to a debilitating refusal of it. As might be expected from the previous chapter, these self-deceptions appear in a variety of guises, some of them more subtle than others. However, in contrast to the previous chapter, if we are to get a grip on the ways in which self-deception appears in his films, we need first to come to some understanding of the phenomenon itself. Self-deception may be a common occurrence, but that doesn't make its working easy to describe in philosophical terms. We would do well to focus on the character of self-deception, both since it is elusive and since reflecting on it will allow us to peer more deeply into the lives of Lonergan's characters. In this discussion we will soon turn away from the traditional psychoanalytic interpretation of the phenomenon that grounds the work of people like Lonergan's parents (assuming they hew to a traditional psychoanalytic model) and toward a more socially embedded one that his films themselves illustrate.

What Is Self-Deception?

Philosophical reflection on self-deception often starts with a paradox. How is it, philosophers ask, that we can deceive ourselves without knowing we are doing so and therefore undercutting the attempt itself? Here's the idea. If we deceive ourselves, it is about something we don't want to see. More significant cases would involve not wanting to see or admit something about who we are, but even cases of not wanting to admit that we were rooting for a losing team in a basketball game we just happened to be watching involve not wanting to see something about what we thought or felt or did. It is the thing we don't want to see or admit to ourselves that we hide from ourselves. But mustn't we already know what we don't want to see in order to hide it from ourselves? Mustn't we recognize that aspect of who we are or what we did as unacceptable in order to want to keep it at bay from our consciousness? And if so, wouldn't it always be too late to perform the self-deception? We would have to know what we seek to hide from ourselves in order to hide it. But if we know it, then how can we hide it from ourselves? Self-deception would seem to always arrive on the scene a little bit too late.

Perhaps the first person to offer a sustained account of self-deception was Sigmund Freud, under the category of repression. One can see the centerpiece of his writings as an attempt to understand the phenomenon: what it is, how it works, and where it comes from. The outlines of the account are familiar to most of us, so we can gloss them quickly here.[2]

On Freud's telling, our ability to deceive ourselves rests on the fact that our minds have both a conscious and an unconscious part (as well as a preconscious part, which is tied to consciousness). Our unconscious is formed through a repression that first takes place—at least for boys—in the Oedipal stage. Roughly, the boy falls in love with the mother, would like to kill his rival the father, becomes afraid that the father will frustrate his project by castrating him, and so hides his Oedipal thoughts in a place where even he can't get at them, that is, by forming an unconscious. (For the record, decades after my first exposure to Freud's thought, I remain stunned that anyone would ever believe this story.) Once the unconscious exists it attracts potentially unacceptable thoughts, often if not always associated either directly or indirectly with the Oedipal scene, and keeps them from conscious awareness. That is why, if a person exhibits debilitating psychological symptoms, a psychoanalyst is required to facilitate the understanding of the source of those symptoms. Because the unconscious resists conscious awareness it is impossible, or at least nearly impossible, for the symptom sufferer to reach into their unconscious in order to develop an awareness of what is generating the symptom.

This account of self-deception, like all accounts, focuses on aspects of who a person is that she would rather not see. In this case it is a matter of having unacceptable thoughts that generate behaviors or symptoms that express those thoughts indirectly and can only be understood through a hermeneutical process involving a psychoanalyst. One might ask why the thoughts need to be expressed at all, even indirectly.

Freud's approach is, at this point, hydraulic: what is unconscious seeks expression in consciousness, it presses upon the mind for expression. However, since the unconscious contents cannot be allowed direct expression, they must find their way into our conscious lives obliquely, through symptoms or behaviors that we ourselves do not understand but that have a relationship—perhaps metaphorical, perhaps metonymical, perhaps some other way—to the content itself.

One might ask here whether, if the Oedipal story is found incredible, the entire Freudian edifice collapses. This does not strike me as being the case. One can believe that there is an unconscious aspect to the mind without believing that it was formed through an Oedipal (or, for girls, an Electra) process in the way Freud posits. There would remain the challenge of accounting for its formation, but that does not by itself impugn a belief in its existence. However, there are problems maintaining the belief itself independent of its origins. As Jean-Paul Sartre points out, and as Freud ratifies, the unconscious requires a censor, something that operates either by pressing unacceptable thoughts into the unconscious or letting acceptable thoughts move from unconscious to conscious awareness. (At some points in his thought Freud insists that all thoughts start in the unconscious and then are evaluated for access to consciousness.[3]) However, there is a logical conundrum here. The censor must be aware of the thoughts it is evaluating. And if so, it must in some way be conscious—it must be aware of what it is doing. But if it is conscious it is already too late for evaluation, so we are back in the dilemma cited at the outset. So, in Sartre's view at least, there cannot be an unconscious part of the mind. His discussion of what he calls "bad faith" is an attempt to account for self-deception without positing the existence of an unconscious.[4]

However, could there not be unconsciousness without a particular part of the mind called the unconscious? Does unconsciousness require an unconscious? Perhaps there is a way of accounting for self-deception that does not demand this. Using the thought of Herbert Fingarette and then Michael Billig, I would like to suggest that there is, and then turn to Lonergan's films to see that account displayed in several of his characters. Fingarette offers a psychological explanation while Billig offers a sociological one; however, the two accounts are complementary rather than contradictory and together they help us grasp the phenomenon of self-deception without falling back into the paradox of knowing what one does not want to know.

Fingarette argues that we should think of self-deception on the model of volition and action rather than cognition and perception. That is to say, instead of asking what we know and what we see, we should ask about what we're doing and not doing when we deceive ourselves. He notes that we have a particular skill, that of what he calls "spelling out." We spell out something when we bring it to conscious awareness. Fingarette points out that most of the time our engagement with the world is unconscious rather than conscious. As he tells us, "Rather than taking explicit consciousness for granted, we must come to take its absence for granted; we must see explicit consciousness as a further exercise of a specific skill for a special reason."[5]

Why is this? The reason is not far to seek. We do so many things as we go through our day that if we had to be consciously aware of them we would become paralyzed. Right now I am typing words on to a page. If I had to be aware of each of the movements of my fingers it would take me forever to get through this paragraph. I'm consciously aware only of what I'm trying to write, while my body is doing all sorts of other things of which I am not aware. Of course, now that I say this I'm more aware of my fingers typing, but still not consciously aware of every movement they make. If I developed an itch, I would not be aware of scratching it, especially if I were really caught up in the writing.

So we can see what Fingarette calls spelling out as a skill that brings to consciousness some of what I may be doing or thinking, a skill that occurs against a background of unconscious engagement in the world. This changes the question of self-deception to one of what one is or is not spelling out for oneself. Instead of asking, "'Does he *really* know?' or 'How can he do all this and not know?' we should ask instead, 'How is he engaged in the world,' and 'Does he express this engagement explicitly?'"[6]

If we approach self-deception this way we can, according to Fingarette, begin to see our way toward an account that avoids the paradox. As we grow up we become involved in different and perhaps even contradictory engagements with the world. Some of these we choose, some we do not. This should not be surprising, since we do not choose the circumstances under which we are raised. We are not mere ciphers for the influences upon us; otherwise we would be incapable of choosing anything other than the strongest influence. But neither can we completely divorce ourselves from our circumstances and the history of our upbringing. There are influences on what we do and who we are—that is, to our engagements in and commitments to aspects of the world—that we cannot succeed, or at least have difficulty, in escaping. We would rather not recognize these engagements, but they are there nevertheless. So instead, when they threaten to come to conscious awareness, we disavow them while avowing others.

> The crux of the matter is this: certain forms of spelling-out are in their implication clear affirmations by a person of his personal identity ... . Analogously, one who disavows an emotion, an intent, a deed, thereby surrenders the authority to speak as one who feels, intends, or does so and so, and he abdicates the authority to speak *for*, that is, to spell-out, the emotion, intent, or deed.[7]

Disavowal, then, is an activity, just as spelling out is. It happens when one is brought face-to-face with aspects of an aspect of one's engagement with the world—an emotion, an intent, a behavior—with which one does not identify. But still, it might be asked, isn't this paradoxical? Mustn't I know what I'm disavowing in order to disavow it? And doesn't that mean that disavowal is still too late? No, I don't. This is for two reasons. One is that, as Fingarette has argued, what is avowed or disavowed are engagements with the world that are often unconscious until they are made conscious. Moreover, when an engagement of mine is made conscious to me, it doesn't come with its own label. It doesn't announce itself as doing *this* or feeling *that*. *What* I am doing, feeling, or intending can be interpreted in different ways, and although the evidence may push me toward an interpretation that I disavow, it doesn't require that interpretation. There are other ways I might account for one or another engagement in the world that would lead me away from something I would prefer not to avow.

Alfred Mele has enumerated a number of strategies through which what Fingarette calls disavowal can take place.[8] We can dismiss some evidence that would point us toward an engagement we would rather not admit as unimportant or misguided; alternatively, we can count some evidence as supporting an engagement that should count against it. ("My colleague doesn't dislike me; his insults are just male jousting, showing that we have a strong bond.") We can focus selectively on some aspects of a situation where others are more important or look for evidence of how to think about ourselves in skewed ways.

Moreover, alongside these strategies of biased interpretation that are motivated by what we would like to see or not see, there are what Mele calls "unmotivated" biases that are part of all attention. In many situations some evidence will appear more vivid than other evidence, depending on how it presents itself. We are also more likely to attend to evidence that presents itself as available to us. (Mele draws on the research of Tversky and Kahneman here: "For example, we may mistakenly believe that the number of English words beginning with *r* greatly outstrips the number having *r* in the third position, because we find it much easier to produce words on the basis of a search for their first letter."[9]) Finally, the well-known phenomenon of confirmation bias pulls all of us to be attentive to evidence that would confirm rather than disconfirm beliefs or hypotheses we already hold.

What pushes us toward these strategies of disavowal (or relatedly of avowal of something false)? Sometimes, as Mele points out, there isn't anything in particular. We see a situation or our way of being in the world and interpret it in a fashion that is favorable to us. But often there is something else in play: anxiety. After all, when we are self-deceived we are often brought face-to-face with evidence that would undermine our view of our engagements with the world. This can happen by way of people telling us that we're wrong about ourselves or through worries about what we're doing or by bits of behavior that don't seem to conform easily to our interpretation of what we're up to. In these situations we become uncomfortable.

We need not, for reasons Fingarette has shown, bring to conscious awareness the source of our discomfort. Anxiety is not a signpost that points in the direction of a way of being we'd rather not acknowledge or avow. Anxiety is different from fear, which has a particular object. Instead, anxiety is more free-floating. Something is off, we feel uncomfortable, and so we move to safety. In cases of self-deception that safety would consist in seeing what we're up to in certain ways rather than others. "No, I'm not being nasty; I'm just offering tough love." "I'm not trying to please my boss—you know I'm a rebellious type. It's just coincidence that we both think this is an important project." "I didn't ignore that old man who had fallen in the street while I was in a hurry to my meeting; the fact is, I was thinking about what I was going to say and so I didn't even see him there."

What we have seen so far is the phenomenon of self-deception as it is lived. There is one more aspect to it, an aspect that is much less often discussed but that helps constitute the kinds of things that are avowed and disavowed, things that are on display in several of Lonergan's films. Ironically, this aspect is presented in a book that offers itself as an update of Freudian thought but that instead overturns some of the very foundations of Freud's views. In *Freudian Repression*, Michael Billig reinterprets repression—often using examples from Freud's own life—as arising from social rather than anthropological causes. Our repression—and therefore our self-deception—is rooted in our social, and specifically socially linguistic, conditions rather than in some universal (for boys, at least) Oedipal complex.

Billig notes that language not only opens topics for discussion through conversation but also has mechanisms for closing off discussion. The common phrase, "Yes, but …," often serves as a way to deflect conversation from one topic to another, as any academic who has made a presentation at a conference comes to learn, often to their dismay. However, in addition to changing to preferred topics, "Yes, but …" can also allow someone to move away from topics that cause anxiety. "Actual repression," Billig says, "rather than being confined to the inner dialogues of the isolated individual, is part of outward social life. Two rhetorical elements are required for successful shifting—whether in external or internal dialogue. First there are the small words of the discontinuity markers, which indicate that such a shift is occurring. The second requirement is another topic to move towards."[10]

But why move away from some topics? What makes them unacceptable? In social conversation, of course, there are norms about this. We often interact with others whom we don't respect, but there is a norm that we not say this openly. We all have thoughts that we know would be embarrassing to express, so we keep them to ourselves. For instance, we are loathe to speak ill of the dead or tell someone his newly grown beard doesn't really enhance his appearance. In addition to these many general social norms, there are norms that are specific to situations or contexts. As we grow up we learn these norms; we learn what and when things can and cannot be said.

Of course we don't all learn the same norms. We are brought up in different families, neighborhoods, regions, and countries. This can—and periodically does—lead to misunderstandings and conflicts. Nevertheless, within these various contexts conversation is framed and often driven by norms of proper expression.

Through learning what can be said and expressed we also learn what can be thought and felt. The movement toward repression, then, does not happen solely inside of us but generally moves from the outside in: we learn social norms of acceptability and unacceptability through conversation and then those norms are integrated into our internal lives. Billig, like Fingarette, recognizes that more happens in our lives than we can possibly remember. So we are taught—often through stories—what is and is not to be remembered. Alongside this we are taught what is and is not to be felt, thought, and recognized in oneself.

Speaking of love, he writes, "Repression ... comes into play when we cannot admit to ourselves that we hold particular loves. What is pushed from consciousness, or avoided, is not a bodily feeling, but a means of interpretation."[11] That bodily feeling may involve love, but it will be accompanied by a feeling of anxiety. Moreover, since, as we have seen, behavior does not come with its interpretation attached, one can always interpret what one has done or felt or even thought in ways that are more socially acceptable or, to be precise, more acceptable to oneself given the social context in which one finds oneself.

Repression, then, and the self-deception that goes with it, is a social phenomenon that is taken up psychologically as we learn to converse and more broadly to interact with one another. And, recalling the insights of Fingarette and Mele, we can understand self-deception as a way of not admitting to ourselves aspects of who we are or what we have done, felt, or thought through interpretations that are available to us even in the face of other, more adequate, although more uncomfortable, interpretations. There are strategies for this, strategies that are often triggered by an anxiety that move us away from certain interpretations even before they can get a grip on our consciousness.

As I mentioned at the outset of this chapter, where there is suffering there is often the temptation for self-deception. This is particularly true when the stakes are high, and, as we have seen, Lonergan sets those stakes high by introducing death into the center of all of his films. Let us turn, then, to the films to see how self-deception operates—or fails to operate—in the characters faced with the suffering of death.

Skirting and Avowing Responsibility

Adolescence is a time of great honesty as well as great self-deception. In this transitional period from childhood to adult life, people are mature enough to see things that are passed over or avoided by those who are older, such as the inanity of war and poverty, the debilitating politics of the work world, the dishonesty of so many personal relationships. At the same time there is often a contradictory impulse toward romanticizing and inflating personal experience into a larger drama than it may really merit. Perhaps we could say that adolescence is like adulthood, only more openly revealing. In discussion with Mead, Lonergan commented that, "You can just see the framework a little better with a teen-ager. Grownups are more settled into who they are going to be and what their place in the world is. Teen-agers are kind of poking around and trying different ways of being, ways of acting."[12]

Lisa Cohen is a full-blown adolescent. She sees clearly that Maretti is avoiding admitting what he knows, whether to himself or to others.

She recognizes the absurdity of the fact that the union will not discipline or fire him because it would complicate current negotiations with the city regarding a labor dispute. She can be brutally honest with her mother. But at the same time she deceives herself in different ways throughout the film, and particularly in relation to Monica Patterson's death.

However, before turning to that more central self-deception it would be worth spending a moment on a marginal, yet poignant, one that appears periodically throughout the film: the self-deception that her father, Karl (played by Lonergan himself), cares deeply about her. In contrast to her more combative behavior with her mother and brother (as well as some of her classmates), Lisa is supplicant with her father. She clearly seeks his affection, and he just as clearly is too self-centered to offer it. Early in the film she calls him. It is soon after the accident, she is still traumatized by what has happened, and her tone reveals that she would like some affection from her father. She does not tell him about the accident, which, in retrospect, seems to be because she is afraid he might be disappointed in her. Instead they talk about a horseback riding trip they are planning; it is in planning for the trip that Lisa noticed Maretti's cowboy hat, leading to the accident that kills Monica. Even in their first phone conversation, the distance between what Lisa seeks and what her father will offer is on display. At the end of their conversation, Lisa tells Karl she loves him. It is a burst of affection, coupled with a subtle sense of pleading for return. Karl hesitates before saying, "Um ... I love you too."

In a later conversation, Karl cancels the horseback riding trip, telling her that he is very pressed, that business is picking up for him, and so it's a bad time. Lisa, although disappointed, does not confront him in the way we see her confront others. She has a project, that of gaining his affection, and she cannot recognize that this is a project that is bound to fail. At one point, in a period of tension with her mother, Lisa tells her that she's thinking of going out and living with her father for a year. Joan, predictably, freaks out, which is the reaction Lisa was looking for. But the fact that Lisa thinks that this is even a possibility her father would entertain shows that she does not recognize the depth of his self-involvement.

Lisa's self-deception here is not an uncommon one, especially in families. Consider the aspects of self-deception I canvassed earlier. Lisa does not need to enter the paradox of telling herself what she does not want to admit. Rather, there are certain family signals about what can and cannot be said. She cannot say to her father—in part because she cannot avow to herself—that he does not really care for her. If that thought were to get near to her, she would become anxious. It is too important for her to feel that he loves her to admit the possibility that his love is, at best, impoverished. And Karl just as surely emits signals that some things are to be discussed and others not, while not admitting, even to himself, what these are signals of. Over the years the conversational practice between them has set certain norms that allow discussion to course along certain routes and not others. It is a game they play, one which leaves her perpetually dissatisfied but at least with the illusion that her father has real affection for her. They're going to go on a horseback riding trip together; and when they don't, it must be for a good reason.

This is why the moment of quiet desperation in which Lisa tells him that she loves him is vexing to him. He doesn't know how to respond, because she, while not crossing a red line, has edged right up to the border. Karl tells her he loves her, because that is what is done in that conversational practice, but his heart is not in it. The social rules dictate what is to be said, but there is a palpable discomfort, one that requires that the phone conversation soon come to an end.

Although there are only a few phone conversations between Lisa and her father, they suggest an aspect of who she is that we might not otherwise see. (Those interactions also have an indirect bearing on the central plot of the film—had Karl not offered to go horseback riding with her, Lisa would likely not have noticed, and would certainly not have been captivated, by Maretti's hat.) But they also have a wider significance. Don't we all know people who deceive themselves about the depth of caring their parents have for them? And don't they do it in much the same way that Lisa did? They don't dare confront the situation because somehow they unconsciously sense how tenuous any affection toward them is, how easily it could be lost. By the same token, they cannot admit to themselves the poverty of affection to which they are already subject. And why not? Because if they are not loved by this person they admire, perhaps it means that they themselves are deficient; they are not really lovable. That possibility cannot but make someone anxious; anything that would bring a person near it would likely motivate disavowal. There is no doubt that if someone raised that possibility to Lisa, she would have denied it with a vigor she generally reserved for her outbursts against her little brother. And so the social forms are respected, the conversations stay on their scripted paths, and when the possibility of recognition appears, as it does when Karl cancels the horseback riding trip, it is covered over with other conversation. A moment in which the script written between them over the years might be changed—as when Lisa tells Karl she loves him—creates a discomfort that must be warded off so that everyone can return to what's on the page.

I have lingered over Lisa and Karl's relationship because, although not the centerpiece of the film, it reveals much about many relationships in which people engage and about the self-deception that accompanies them. However, the central thread of the film—Lisa's attempt to hold Maretti responsible—reveals other moments of self-deception, moments that display Lisa's adolescence and yet can find resonance in adults watching *Margaret*.

The primary path Lisa's self-deception takes lies in her complicated relationship with Maretti. Although, as we have seen, she only has one short direct interaction with him after the accident, much of the film is taken up with her attempt to hold him responsible. The first self-deception, though, takes place immediately after the accident, and it involves a seeming collusion with him. When she is questioned by the police at the scene of the accident, Lisa says that she guesses the light was still green when Maretti crossed the intersection but then isn't quite sure. As Lonergan unfolds the scene there is an invitation to the viewer to participate in this self-deception. As I mentioned earlier, the accident is characterized by fast cuts among several points of view. One of those points of view appears to be from Lisa's perspective of the light turning red. However, because everything unfolds so quickly it is possible for the viewer to doubt this—not that the light turned red, which is made clear to the viewer, but that Lisa saw it turn red. Then, during the interview, she sees Maretti looking at her from a distance as he is talking to another police officer about his perspective.

This is a complicated moment in the film. During their conversation later, Lisa insists to Maretti that they were in collusion in both insisting the light was still green when they both knew it wasn't. But that itself seems like a self-deception. At the moment of the interview, Lisa appears confused and uncertain about what she saw. This would of course be understandable, given the traumatic character of what has just unfolded. But even then, the stakes are clear. If the light had turned red, then she was a participant in causing Monica Patterson's death. As Billig tells us, there is a deep relationship between what we are supposed and not supposed to think and feel and say, given particular social norms, and what we can admit to ourselves. There was something, then, pushing her toward denying what we, the viewers, think she saw. It is not hard to imagine Lisa convincing herself at that moment that she did not see the light turn red and that, therefore, it must still have been green. (She also said she was running to catch the bus, which she may have known was a lie—although it is not entirely certain that she wasn't just trying to convince herself of something in the moment—but which in any event indicates her concern that what she did was participate in causing Monica Patterson's death.)

One might want to argue here that at this moment Lisa is not self-deceived, she is just lying about the light as she was about trying to catch the bus. That would imply that she always knew she was lying and that she really did believe that she and Maretti were in collusion about the accident. Such an interpretation would be in keeping with the romantic aspect of adolescence—there was, in her mind, a deep bond produced between them through his look that led them on a path together toward a cover-up. I don't believe that evidence tilts decisively toward either interpretation, and that itself is significant, showing that the distinction between self-deception and lying can periodically be a porous one. However, because of her confusion and upset during the interview, I find it less plausible that she reflected on the situation and decided consciously to lie about the light rather than engaging in a momentary self-deception that would allow her to exit the situation with less guilt.

Nevertheless, Lisa soon recognizes that she did not tell the police the truth during that initial interview. So she is implicated in Monica's death. This is where the attempt to hold Maretti responsible becomes a central prop in her self-deception, one that, as we saw, falls apart when it becomes clear in the attorney's negotiation with Abigail and her husband that Maretti is not going to be accorded any responsibility. In sorting out this self-deception—as with many self-deceptions— we should be careful in seeking to understand it. It is not that Lisa denies her responsibility for the accident; rather, she just focuses elsewhere. It is Maretti's culpability that she seeks to have recognized. That is to say, she looks outward rather than inward; or better, she looks outward in order not to have to look inward. Fingarette tells us that in self-deception, "One mark of disavowal is the high degree of disavowed engagement is isolated from the influence of everything that is avowed."[13] It is as though, in her quest to have Maretti publicly acknowledged as responsible, Lisa engages in a disavowal by isolating her own participation from the rest of her behavior—that is, until she can no longer do so.

How shall we understand this moment of Lisa's avowal of responsibility? Recall first Maretti's own denial of responsibility. It's unclear whether or not there is self-deception at play in it, since we don't see him for very long. He spends a good bit of the short conversation confronting Lisa with the weaknesses in her own story, especially her already having told the police that the light was green.

Near the end of the scene he adds that nobody can help the dead woman in any case and he has a family to take care of and then asks her whether she's prepared to take care of his family if they put him in jail. This might indicate that he has some awareness of what he's done, but that remains uncertain. Fingarette argues that, "Isolation, non-responsibility, and the ability to spell-out, with the consequences in turn attendant upon these, constitute the three chief dimensions of disavowal, three profoundly significant defects of personal integrity."[14] (We will later raise the question of whether disavowal is always a defect of personal integrity.) On the one hand, it seems that Maretti does all three; on the other hand, spelling out is something one does with oneself, and it is unclear to whom he is refusing to spell out his involvement in the accident, himself or just Lisa.

In any event, the upshot of this is that Lisa knows he will not accept any responsibility for the accident. So she initiates her efforts to have him fired.

Later, when it becomes clear at the end of the negotiations that the legal strategy won't work either, since Abigail and her husband are interested only in the money and the attorney insists both that this is the best deal they're going to get and that Abigail, as the next of kin, has authority over the negotiations, Lisa cracks. She is thrown back on herself in recognizing that Maretti will neither take responsibility nor be held to it. He will not assume any blame nor will he be held to account. But Lisa knows—she has long admitted it to herself and others—that he ran the red light. And she also knows that he did it while she distracted him by asking about the cowboy hat. She has spent much of her time since the accident focused on Maretti's culpability as a way of neglecting her own. And so at that moment she has nothing else to fall back on; she is alone with the event and her own participation in it. Maretti is going to be out of the picture. He can walk away, at least as far as she is concerned. That leaves only her and the guilt she has been warding off in her quest to have him fired. Since there is nowhere else to turn, she turns back upon herself. "I'm the one who killed her! I'm the one who killed her! But at least I know I did it, and that guy has no idea! And he's wandering around blaming everybody else and all I want is for somebody to let him know that what he did was wrong!"

In her quest to hold Maretti responsible, Lisa engages in all the aspects of self-deception that we have canvassed. Throughout much of the film she disavows her participation in the death, not by denial but by focusing on Maretti's responsibility and, when she turns toward herself, on her failure to report truthfully his going through the red light rather than her participation in the accident. She engages in the strategies Mele describes as focusing or attending selectively to certain aspects of the situation and, relatedly, selective evidence gathering. Moreover, because she is an adolescent with heightened emotional responses, her engagement in these strategies is on fuller display, more enthusiastically pursued, than it might be with an adult—as is her moment of recognition and confession.

Finally, the social pressure for her to find herself innocent of the death of Monica Patterson is obvious. There are very few places in the world, if any, where one would not want to find oneself guiltless of participation in the accidental death of another. She is not in a situation—as Lee Chandler is—that might be beyond the question of social norms; she did not cause the death of her children or even of anyone she knew. Social norms had a role to play in her situation, but perhaps one so obvious that they did not need calling attention to. In other cases, the social norms constraining one's relation to a death might be less obvious, although perhaps more pervasive. This is the case with Sammy and Terry Prescott in the small town of Scottsville.

Self-Deception and Social Norms

There's nothing like a small town to box one in with social norms. In a larger city there are always places to escape to. Even in cities that are composed of different neighborhoods where each feels like its own town, a person can always escape from one neighborhood to another one with different norms or at least absent oneself from a particular neighborhood for a while. In rural areas, where the norms may be just as binding as in small towns, there is always the option of lessening social interaction. In small towns, however, wherever you go there are people that see what you're doing; your behavior is always surveilled. For kids this often results in reports to their parents from prying neighbors or other townspeople. For adults it can be a constant reminder that there is disapproval waiting at the borders of a narrow range of acceptable behavior.

These normative constraints often leave people who live in small towns with three options. The first, of course, is conformity. One can accede to the norms and surrender oneself to the required demeanor and conduct. Usually this is done not as a conscious renunciation of other ways of living but instead slowly and gradually and, most important for our purposes, unconsciously. The molding happens as a piecemeal daily wearing down of other options and a reinforcement of the norms of acceptable behavior. It's not just that you are forced to be someone you constantly fight against. Often it's the opposite: you identify with the ways in which you are molded. This is no surprise. The cognitive dissonance of constant struggle against constraints can leave one exhausted and depressed. At the margins, if the molding is effective, one can become one of the very monitors of the social norms.

The second option is flight. The norms become too much, one becomes an outsider, and one leaves. Small towns are often hemorrhaging people, often their most talented or creative people, because they refuse to submit to the required normative constraints. This is not to say that everyone who abandons a small town in the face of its normative straightjacket is creative or intelligent. *Anyone* who cannot fit in will be tempted to leave. However, among those who do leave will likely be those who would open novel possibilities if they stayed—and in doing so challenge the current normative structure.

The final option is to stay and often be marginalized. It is perhaps the most difficult path and is not often chosen. The face of constant disapproval is a harsh one to have gazing upon one. Very few people can stand it, and Lonergan doesn't offer us an example in *Count*.

He also doesn't offer us a number of examples of the constraints of a small town in any overt way, at least in this film. (In *Manchester*, the anger of townspeople toward Lee Chandler could not be more obvious. We'll return to this below.) The presentation of constraints is more subtle. When Sammy shouts at Terry over lunch in the restaurant the camera pans back to see the whole restaurant pause and stare at them. When Terry gets off the bus in Scottsville, as we have seen, the first conversation he has is with the police officer who announced his parents' death to Sammy earlier. That fact reinforces the stagnant normative character of the town. Moreover, their conversation reminds Terry—and the audience—of the town's normative structure. When Terry tells the officer, "Keep enforcing the peace," he replies, "Well, that will be a little harder now that you're home, but I'll do what I can." When Brian shows up to manage the bank he concedes that the bank is a small-town one but that he would like it to function like a bank in a larger town. (To be sure, in this case he introduces new and more constraining norms, but is met with the resistance of those for whom a set of norms are already in place.) The camera periodically focuses on the town's main street, which is often bereft of people, emphasizing its smallness and isolation. Finally, Terry's conversation with Sammy's son Rudy at night harps on the town's constraints and the need for Rudy to leave when he gets older because there's nothing for him there.

Sammy, of course, picks the first path, the path of conformity. This path does not require self-deception. It's possible for a person to say to herself, "I recognize the constraints of living like this and I accept them." It probably doesn't happen often, because, as mentioned, the work of those constraints is more gradual and unconscious. But it can happen. In Sammy's case, however, that's not how it works. Sammy needs the self-deception. This is not only because of the constraints themselves, but more deeply because her own emotional turmoil is constantly threatening to break out against them. In the face of norms whose disapproval is always hovering there is an inner unrest, an unrest that is traceable back to the death of her parents, and that can burst out at any moment.

We have seen the surface of this struggle in Sammy's attempt to make sure everything is okay, both through her beckoning smile and her asking for ratification that she and her lovers are still friends. But why must this be a struggle? And what makes it self-deception? We get a hint of the answer to these questions over a dinner shared by Terry, Sammy, and Rudy. Terry comments to Rudy that his mother was a much wilder woman when she was younger, and Rudy turns to her and asks whether this was true. Her response is, "No comment." So the abandon that Terry elicits from his sister is not *ex nihilo*. There are roots to it, roots that have been layered over by a conformity to the norms of her small town.

The other place we see the source of struggle is in the abandon itself. What could be more transgressive of the norms of a place like Scottsdale than an affair? It's not that small towns don't contain plenty of people who have affairs. Moreover, it is doubtless that many of those affairs come from boredom at the conformity to which those people are subject. Nevertheless, in the threat they pose to the stability of a town's relationships, affairs are considered shameful in the normative structure of small towns. (To be sure, they are generally frowned upon in larger cities as well, but not because they pose any threat to the relational structures within those cities.) Sammy's willingness to engage in an affair shows a side of her, one that is brought out in Terry's visit, that is often denied—or better suppressed—in other aspects of her life. Recall here Lonergan's claim that, "Her problems are so buried and his so out in the open it's a lot easier for her to deal with his problems than with hers."

In fact, Sammy is, at the prospect of Terry's visit, even in self-denial about his problems. When she learns through his letter that he's coming to visit, she is overjoyed. Her smile when reading the letter is different from her "everything is okay, isn't it?" smile with which she seeks to ward off conflict or discomfort. It lights up her whole face, including her eyes, which, in the other smile, are more pleading than joyful. In her elation Sammy does not recognize what will become obvious when Terry visits: that he is going to bring chaos into her world, a chaos that will culminate in taking Rudy to visit his father, whose existence Sammy has more or less denied throughout Rudy's life and who, it turns out, has no desire to see his son.

Sammy's joy at Terry's arrival is unmitigated, mindless of the emotional baggage that Terry brings with him and spreads across her life, no doubt every time he visits. In a different way from that of her relationship with the various people of Scottsville, Sammy hides from herself the disruption that is never far from her and that cannot ultimately be contained or subdued.

Sammy is in a struggle she does not see and would likely deny it if it were presented to her. It is a struggle that is grounded on the death of her parents and structured by the norms of her community. Lonergan comments that, "She defends against the death while Terry just says fuck it to everything." Sammy would, at least as far as she knows, live a life of tranquility, structured by her activities and guided by her religion. But this is not all of who Sammy is; Terry's visit reveals this to us in the audience more than to her.

But what of Terry himself? Is he not also in some form of self-deception, perhaps of a very different sort from Sammy? Lonergan describes him as a "thoughtful screwup," which might lead us to think so. However, if we ask the question too generally, that is, if we pose the question as one of whether Terry is in self-deception, the answer is bound to be yes. This is not for any deep or special reason. Rather, it is that all of us, in one way or another, are in self-deception.

There are aspects of who we are or what we are doing that we would have trouble admitting to ourselves. Whether it is being less socially aware than we would like to think ourselves to be or seeking approval from our boss when we think ourselves independent of such things or driven by fear of failure when we would prefer to see ourselves as go-getters or even just rooting for a team we've just started watching a moment ago when we would like to think that we're just relaxing in front of the television. So the question really should be whether Terry, like Sammy, is engaged in a form of self-deception that is importantly structuring his life.

On the surface it might seem that the answer is here no. After all, Terry, in contrast to Sammy, has rejected the town's norms. He has taken the second path in relation to small-town norms described above. He despises Scottsville and cannot abide spending any significant amount of time in it. It is not that we should take Terry as psychologically healthy. He is clearly immature and we are meant to see him, like Sammy, as damaged by his parents' death. He just as clearly exhibits terrible judgment, as exemplified by his taking Rudy to see a father that Sammy was does not want Rudy to see and that Sammy is wise in keeping him from seeing. But there are many ways of being damaged; damage through a debilitating self-deception is only one. Perhaps Terry has escaped that particular form of damage.

I believe, however, that Terry is deceiving himself in a way that is structuring for his life and, moreover, that that self-deception is rooted in his experience with the town's norms as well as with his parents' death. Because, as we have seen, we do not know the specific elements of Terry's (or Sammy's) histories between the time of their parents' death and the present moment of the film, what I am going to say here is bound to be a bit speculative. However, even though the case is more obvious with Sammy, I think we can make out such a case with Terry as well, a case that would not be unfamiliar to many of us since we also can see it in other people we might know.

To put it bluntly, Terry's life is largely structured through his rejection of a set of social norms and his failure to recognize that rejection for what it is. Or, to state it another way, Terry takes himself as having rejected Scottsville's norms when in fact he is bound to them through the project of continually running away from them. His life, as we know, is defined by wandering and by an inability to engage himself in long-term commitments (except for the love of his sister, even where that is often expressed in unhelpful ways). He travels as far away from Scottsville as he can—Alaska and Florida, among other places. But there is no place he can settle down. He tells Rudy in that conversation at night how important it is to leave the town so that Rudy does not wind up like his sister. However, Terry himself is always in the process of leaving Scottsville. If he has a life project, that would be it. He thinks that he has left the town when in fact he is never done leaving it. If Sammy is bound to Scottsville's norms by way of their constraint even though they leave her in unrest, Terry is bound to the same norms by way of a constant rebellion, one that he cannot finish in order to commit to something other than that rebellion itself. This is why he seems too immature. He has not left a form of adolescent rebellion and is not likely to any time soon. In the voice-over to *Count*, Lonergan comments that, "Everyone in the movie is struggling against the constraints they find themselves in." I would argue, especially in Terry's and Sammy's case—although it is often true of the other characters as well—that those constraints, following Billig, are socially grounded, and at least for the brother and sister they are largely the same constraints. It is just that they have created opposite struggles for them.

The idea that a person's life can be largely structured by a rebellion they can neither complete nor abandon should not be an unfamiliar one to many of us. Sometimes it is parental constraints that become the source of such rebellion. Someone drinks too much because her parents were controlling teetotalers or joins the army and introduces strict discipline into every corner of his life because of household chaos. At other times it is social constraints that motivate the rebellion, whether these be confining religious strictures or political ideologies or a class emphasis on what constitutes proper behavior. What characterizes all of these rebellions, however, is that they never end. They never develop into positive alternative projects or commitments and so they leave the people who engage in them defined by what they are against. This often develops into a form of nagging resentment of the kind we also see in Terry Prescott. Something is always wrong, someone always against him, making him the victim of a world he cannot control. That is why, when he breaks the social norms by bringing Rudy to a bar to play pool late at night or taking him to see his father, it is always with a sense of going against burdensome norms rather than foresight into the positive effects of what might emerge. (If he had considered the latter, no doubt he would at least not have taken Rudy for the visit with his father.)

In their different ways, then, both Sammy and Terry deceive themselves in relation to a set of social norms that, while playing a central role in configuring their lives, rarely if ever appear in their overt consciousness—or even overtly in the film. They are hinted at in *Count*'s unfolding in much the way they are in their behavior. This is usually the way self-deception works: through gaps or symptoms or details or small incoherencies in a person's way of being rather than through obvious signals that would be easier to confront and harder for the actor herself to miss. However, what about when, in the face of tragedy, there is a failure of self-deception? When what has happened cannot be shunted aside, minimized, or even momentarily escaped?

The Failure of Self-Deception

As we have emphasized throughout this book, Lonergan's films test his characters against one form or another of death. The harshest test, we know, is reserved for Lee Chandler, the man who causes the death of his children. It is a test that never stops defining him.

It also never stops defining the relation to him of the town in which he lived. This latter is a point brought home to the viewer several times in the film. When Lee arrives back in *Manchester by the Sea* to pick up Patrick after Patrick's father (and Lee's brother) has died, he walks into a high school ice hockey practice where Patrick is playing for the team. The coach asks who he is, and the other players inform him that he's Patrick's uncle. "That's Lee Chandler?" the coach asks. "*The* Lee Chandler?" Immediately before that, when Lee had called the vice principal's office to let him know he was on his way to pick up Patrick, the vice principal tells his assistant that it was Lee on the phone and the assistant asks incredulously, "*Lee Chandler?*" The name—the full name—has a single association, one to which, in the view of many people in the town, Lee's life is reduced—as it is in his own eyes. Moreover, as we have seen, Lee has trouble finding work in the town because of this association.

Unlike Terry Prescott, however, Lee is not in rebellion against the town's norms, mostly because he identifies with them. He does not deceive himself about what many in Manchester think of him. Quite the opposite, he identifies with their view and with their rejection of him. It would be inaccurate to say that he identifies with that view *because* it is their view. His view of himself does not derive from the town's social norms or their view of him. He hardly needs those norms or that view to live in the shadow of what he has done. The momentousness of Lee's act (or omission) places him beyond the reach of the norms Billig cites. It also, and relatedly, places him beyond the reach of self-deception. Lee can survive the moment that now defines him, but it is survival and nothing more that he is capable of. In an interview after *Manchester* appeared (included in the DVD version of the film), Lonergan comments that, "He's working all the time at things that the rest of us don't have to work at," and, "He's a guy who's trying to keep the walls from caving in every single day of his life." Lee keeps himself together, barely, but it takes all his effort to go through a day bearing the weight of his failure to replace the screen in front of the fireplace one drunken night when he decided to go to the store.

The "barely" qualifier comes out in a couple of ways during the film. First, there are the fights. The first night we see Lee, he is, after a difficult day's work, at a bar. He is drunk and comes to think that he is being stared at by two customers across the way, so he wanders over and picks a fight with them. Later in the film, after his unexpected conversation with Randy, he picks another fight at a bar in Manchester when a customer happens to bump shoulders with him as he's passing through. Both fights seem, on the surface, arbitrary and unmotivated. But in each case there are preceding causes that reveal Lee's fragility. In the first case there is a difficult day: a woman has accused him of wanting to see her naked, he swears at her, and he is subsequently dressed down by his boss. In the second case, of course, there is the conversation with Randy. Both fights, along with the triviality of their precipitants and the nature of their causes, reveal Lee's difficulty in holding himself together. He carries with him an explosive anger that is mostly directed toward himself but, given the proper circumstances, can be shifted outward toward others.

The other way the "barely" is displayed is through his relationship, or better nonrelationship, with women in the film. On the night of the first fight, preceding the fight, Lee is approached by a woman at the bar. After accidentally spilling part of her drink on his clothes, she starts to flirt with him. Lee neither flirts back nor engages in conversation. He more or less just sits there, allowing an awkwardness to settle in between them until she turns away. Later, invited to the home of one of Patrick's girlfriends, Lee sits in silence with the girlfriend's mother while the two younger people are upstairs. Eventually the mother goes upstairs, knocking on the door and disturbing the couple as they are preparing themselves for sex, telling them that she can't engage him in conversation. "He won't talk," she says, "I realize I'm not the most fascinating person in the world, but it's very, very strained."

We know from scenes of Lee's past that he was once warm and outgoing. The contrast between his present state and his past one could not be starker. In the voice-over, Lonergan notes that Lee won't let himself talk to women, that he'd rather allow the discomfort than engage with them. This, it seems to me, is because of the emotional stakes involved. To become socially engaged with a woman is to allow the possibility of intimacy back into his life. Lee cannot permit this, probably because he feels he does not deserve it, and moreover because to allow that intimacy would be an act of disloyalty to his family—or at least to the memory of his family. He refuses to allow himself any of the emotional warmth that was once at the center of his life with Randy and his kids as well as with Joe and Patrick. It is not so much that he is so tightly wound that emotional engagement would threaten to unravel him, to break the dam of his emotions—although there is probably some of that as well. More centrally, Lee does not merit emotional warmth or acceptance. He is beneath all that, unfit for human connection.

And here we arrive at the heart of the matter: far from deceiving himself about what he has done, Lee is incapable of deceiving himself. He cannot let go of the incident, nor even blunt any of the sharp edges that are continually cutting into him from it. It is a gaping wound whose pain cannot—will not—be blunted. It might seem obvious that it should be this way, and to Lee it is obvious. However, the film does offer him ways to lessen the pain through smaller or larger self-deceptions, none of which he is willing to adopt. As we have seen, in the interview the morning after the fire, the fire marshal tells him, "You made a horrible mistake. Like a million other people did last night. But we don't wanna crucify you. It's not a crime to leave the screen off the fireplace." It was misfortune, the rolling of a log on to the floor, that likely caused the tragedy. The fire marshal offers him a way to minimize, or at least rationalize, what has happened.

Moreover, the fact that he was using the fireplace rather than the central heating was an expression of care for Randy, whose sinuses dry out with the central heat. A less caring person, particularly when drunk, and more particularly after he has been yelled at by his wife in front of his friends, would be less likely to take his wife's preferences into account.

Finally, it's not even certain that a log rolled out of the fireplace. When Lee recounts his night to the fire marshal and the police, he says that that's what must have happened. He wasn't there, and so couldn't be sure. It's possible that it was something else that did it, perhaps a spark that might have burst out over the screen even if it had been there. Or perhaps his memory is mistaken and he did replace the screen. After all, he was drunk at the time.

Lee is having none of this, not during the interview with the police and not after. Not at any point in his life. He allows nothing to blunt the impact of this single idea: he caused the death of his children, he caused their burning to death. Instead of disavowal Lee is engaged in an ongoing and brutal avowal with which he haunts himself nearly every waking hour. He makes self-deception entirely impossible for himself.

One might object here that the self-deception is in fact in refusing to take account of these mitigating factors. Mele discusses cases of what he calls "twisted self-deception" in which people deceive themselves into thinking that they—or things in their world—are worse than what they would like to think of themselves. The classic case is that of jealousy, in which "avoiding falsely believing that their spouses are faithful may be so important to some people that they test the relevant hypothesis in ways that are less likely to lead to a false belief in a spouses' fidelity than to a false belief in their spouses' infidelity."[15]

This, however, would be incorrect in Lee Chandler's case. He is not missing anything, nor is he twisting the facts to make the situation appear worse than it is. It is all quite as bad as he considers it to be. We might wonder why he cannot let this go, but that is different from ascribing self-deception. And even so, our wondering this is not required or necessarily even suggested. It is just as difficult—perhaps more difficult—to imagine moving on in one's life in full recognition of having done (or again not done) what Lee Chandler has done as it is to wonder why one is not moving on.

There is a lesson here about self-deception, one that is not always adequately noted in contemporary philosophies of self-deception. The tendency is to speak of self-deception as though it were always a bad thing. For instance, Fingarette, as we have seen, calls the aspects of disavowal "profoundly significant defects of personal integrity." However, this is not always the case. Perhaps Lee could use a little more self-deception, even if it is only to blunt the force of his responsibility for what has occurred. Perhaps a bit of doubt about whether it was the log that rolled onto the floor or a more vivid perception of why he did not use the central heat would allow him to go on about his life in a slightly less tortured way. I think we would hesitate to call small moves in one direction or another like that "profoundly significant defects of personal integrity." Or, if we did, we would be hesitant to condemn them. Lee's pain is an expression, however futile, of his caring for his children, an expression the audience was privy to in the flashbacks of the film. Self-deception, for Lee, might have been a way of personal coping rather than personal irresponsibility.

This is not to say that it would have been easy for him to deceive himself. In Lee's case, because of his character and history, it may have been impossible. That is a speculation I'm hesitant to make. My point, rather, is that, were he capable of some modest self-deception here, it might not have been a "defect" or at least not a bad thing for him.

There is a wider point in the neighborhood, one I can only gesture at without straying too far from the film itself. Self-deception is something we all do at different points in our lives. After all, as Fingarette notes, our unconscious engagement in the world is wider—necessarily so—than our conscious engagement. There are probably aspects of who each of us is that we do not avow to ourselves. And this is not always a problem, something to be overcome. There may be aspects to a person whose disavowal does not cause disruption for them or for those around them. In fact, it may be the opposite. There can be self-deceptions, for instance that one is insecure about one's abilities in a particular area, whose existence allows one to go on more adequately than one otherwise would. After all, most of our projects in life do not require complete self-transparency. Instead they require that we get on with them as best as we can, bringing our flaws both known and unknown with us, creating our trajectory in a world fraught with its own flaws.

Conclusion

Self-deception is often a temptation. It can be motivated by many different aspects of our experience, but it is most tempting when we are in the presence of facets of ourselves that we would rather not acknowledge or avow. Those facets can be revealed in our suffering, and in particular in our suffering in relation to death.

However, the temptation of self-deception is not solely an individual thing. It is bound to the norms of the societies we inhabit. For the most part we suffer from facets of ourselves that violate social norms, or at least would if we allowed them to be seen—even to ourselves. So we hide those facets from ourselves and from others. Lisa Cohen hides her guilt for the participation in causing the death of Monica Patterson from herself until she can no longer. Sammy Prescott hides her struggle against the constraints of Scottsville behind her smile and her religion while Terry hides his inability to move on behind his anger and resentment toward those same constraints.

This is where what some think of as the paradox of self-deception arises. How can we hide uncomfortable facets of ourselves from ourselves without knowing we are doing so? However, as we have seen, there is no real paradox here. The human mind is a capacious thing, more unconscious than conscious. Anxiety protects us from spelling out to ourselves some of what is unconscious, while avowal and disavowal and their related strategies do the conscious work of maintaining a view of ourselves that is preferable for us to have.

As always with Lonergan's films, the depth and the complexity of his characters and the fine-grained specificity of their circumstances resist sweeping conclusions at the same time they offer us glimpses into the human condition. Lisa Cohen's self-deception is not Sammy or Terry Prescott's, and each of theirs is not the other's. And, as we have seen and will see again, each of them is a "full human being." They are not reducible to their self-deceptions; they are always more than those.

Sometimes, however, self-deception is not an option. When someone causes the death of his children by fire, and through his own negligence, perhaps he must be exiled to a territory beyond self-deception. It is no longer available to him. And this, too, teaches us something. Self-deception, often derided in discussions of it, is not always an aspect of ourselves to be overcome, not even to the limited extent to which we may be capable of it. The goal of knowing who we are or of admitting to ourselves who we are, while important in many cases, has its limits. If the Delphic mantra is "Know thyself," perhaps it ought to be modified into the less pithy but more accurate, "Know thyself to the extent that thou can do so and still go on." After all, we are creatures with emotional limits as well as epistemic ones. There is only so much we can take before we crack. Lee Chandler, who stands on the far side of self-deception, reminds us of this.

The rejection of Nietzsche's aphorism and the discussion of self-deception in Lonergan's films have revealed the intricate character of our lives by illustrating them with examples at the extreme of death. In doing so, they have challenged simple or wholesale philosophical pronouncements upon our human character. It will be no surprise, then, to discover that among the complexities of these characters—and of ourselves—is a normative complexity that resists any clean and uncomplicated moral judgment. We turn now to that investigation.

4

Normative Complexity

In our assessment of the world and the people in it, there are many types of values we might invoke. There are aesthetic values of beauty and harmony, political values of freedom and equality, athletic values of strength and grace, conversational values of wit and interest, intellectual values of intelligence and curiosity, and many more. In evaluating people and their actions, however, one set of values is usually placed above all others: moral values. People are said to be better or worse based on the moral appraisal of what they do or who they are. Everything else tends to be, although not an afterthought, at least relegated to second place. Other values must wait in the wings until a moral judgment is passed; they can provide supplementary assessment afterward.

Nowhere is this idea more prominently on display than in philosophy. The three major strains of philosophical thought about ethics—virtue theory, deontology, and consequentialism—all posit the centrality of moral values in structuring a human life. And the two fundamental tasks of moral theory—to offer future guidance and retrospective assessment—seek to offer us the fundamental framework for evaluating who we are or what we do.

That evaluation does not occur in the same way in ancient moral theories as it does in modern ones. Roughly put, ancient theories ask a different question from that asked by modern ones.[1] For the ancients, the key question is one of who one should be or how one should live.[2] For the moderns, by contrast, the question is one of how one should act. This difference is sometimes marked by calling the ancient theories ethical and the modern ones moral. However we mark it, though, the differences are not trivial.

For the ancients, and here Aristotle can stand as a primary example, the question of who one should be or how one should live is a question of how to fashion and conduct a life. Lives have trajectories, they unfold over time. They are not made up of a series of unrelated actions but rather should be conceived as diachronic wholes, or at least in terms of long chronological stretches. (One might, for instance, distinguish childhood from adulthood for the purposes of ethical education and assessment.) In Aristotle's case, this requires the development of particular virtues, virtues whose expression constitutes a flourishing life. Virtues such as courage, magnanimity, truthfulness, and good temper are the themes that characterize an excellent human life, a life that is achieving its proper telos or goal. The point of being human is to develop and express these virtues; conversely, a human life can be judged in accordance with how well developed those virtues are.[3]

Modern moral theories, by contrast, focus primarily on acts rather than on lives. To be sure, there is often a reference to virtuous living in these theories. But the point of such living is not the life itself but rather that living virtuously will prompt correct moral action, and it is the latter that is ultimately the locus of guidance and assessment. Where the two major modern moral theories diverge is on the question of whether, in accordance with deontology, the proper locus is on the intention or the means of an action, or instead, in accordance with consequentialism, on the act's consequences.

For deontologists, and here we might take the eighteenth-century philosopher Immanuel Kant as emblematic, a moral act is one that is animated by the right intention. Simply put, a correct act will accord with what he calls the Categorical Imperative, which he offers in four different formulations. The first one, the Formula of Universal Law, states, "Act only on that maxim through which you can at the same time will that it should become a universal law."[4] For Kant, the Categorical Imperative is not simply a guide to a certain kind of action. It reflects what is the highest and most important task of human living, the expression of a good will. For Kant, "It is impossible to conceive anything at all in the world, or even out of it, which can be taken as good without qualification, except a *good will*."[5] What is absolutely good in human (or any rational being's) action is the expression of good will; good will, in turn, is expressed by acting on the basis of the Categorical Imperative. (For Kant, this involves not merely acting in accordance with the Imperative—which can happen from a variety of motives—but acting out of respect for the moral law itself.)

By contrast, for consequentialists what is at issue in moral action is not the intention but rather the outcome. Here we can refer to the utilitarian John Stuart Mill as our exemplar. For Mill, the ultimate goal of human action should be to produce the greatest amount of overall happiness (or, to be more exact, the greatest sum of happiness over unhappiness). Now it may be asked how to conceive this happiness; utilitarians have disputed this question since its inception.

For Mill's predecessor, Jeremy Bentham, happiness is just the sum total of pleasure. Mill himself, however, considered that there were two types of pleasures, a higher and a lower one. How could one tell the difference? Through experience. "Of two pleasures, if there be one to which all or almost all who have experience of both give a decided preference, irrespective of any feeling of moral obligation to prefer it, that is the more desirable pleasure."[6] Nevertheless, whether higher or lower or simply more or less, the right course of action is always the one that provides the most pleasure, happiness, utility, or whatever, once all the calculations are in.

What deontologists and consequentialists share with each other, as well as with their ancient brethren and sisters, is that the highest form of life or action is moral or ethical. The moral and the ethical may be defined differently, in terms of a life, an intention, or an outcome, but all of these theories across the history of Western philosophy share the idea that the highest values, however conceived, are ethical or moral values.[7]

There is something compelling about this idea. Inasmuch as we take the well-being of ourselves and our fellow humans (and perhaps fellow creatures more broadly) to be a central concern, the values associated with the moral and the ethical rightly stand as a requirement of our consideration. Ask yourself whether in order to have the works of Shakespeare we would need to kill an innocent child. We might think of the works of Shakespeare as among the most significant expressions of human art; nevertheless, how many of us would be prepared to sacrifice the life of a child in order to retain them? The very thought is unimaginable to most of us, an indication of the role morality plays in our lives. In fact, it seems that if we are to cross a moral boundary it can only be for the reason that what lies on the other side of the ledger is also moral. If, for instance, torture is ever permissible (a position I am not endorsing), it must be that it saves enough other lives to justify it. One can no more torture someone to save Shakespeare's works than to allow the death of a child for them.

It may well be that one or another of these moral theories offers us the best framework to guide and assess our behavior. And, because the history of humankind does not provide much hope that we can act rightly just trusting our unaided instincts, they may be a necessary aspect of decent human living. However, these theories also threaten to blind us to the normative complexity of human life. By "normative complexity" here I would like to understand two things. First, the moral is only one register of the norms by which we judge ourselves and others. What is good or bad, broadly speaking, in a life cannot be seen solely through a moral or ethical lens. There are other normative lenses we must adopt if we are to do justice to our assessments of our human compatriots.

For the moment let me offer just one example.[8] In addition to moral values, we may judge a life (ours as well as others) from the perspective of what might be called "narrative values." There are certain ways of living that attract our admiration or prick our imagination, even if those ways of living are not accounted for on a moral register. Think, for instance, of the intensity of a rock singer or a mountain climber. Or consider the curiosity of a seeker after knowledge or the spirituality of certain (non-proselytizing) religious folks. Values like these can characterize a life without necessarily being moral ones, values that concern how we *ought to* live or treat others. In fact, it may be that such narrative values can often conflict with moral ones without losing all of their normative force. The artist whose intense commitment to her work leads her to neglect the needs of others would be a classic example. On the one hand we may be repelled by that neglect or even callousness; yet on the other we might concede that there is nevertheless something admirable in their commitment (as long as it does not involve torturing others or causing the death of children).

We might even go further. The philosopher Susan Wolf, to whose work we will return later in this chapter, argues in her article "Moral Saints" that most of us would not even want to live in a world populated solely by those who are entirely morally upstanding. For her,

> Given the empirical circumstances of our world, it seems to be an ethical fact that we have unlimited potential to be morally good, and endless opportunity to promote moral interests. But this is not incompatible with the not-so-ethical fact that we have sound, compelling, and not particularly selfish reasons to choose not to devote ourselves univocally to realizing this potential or taking up this opportunity.[9]

Why not? Because there are other values, nonmoral values, that are worth expressing alongside the moral ones. A person might, in one of her examples, seek to become an Olympic swimmer or a concert pianist. These are not moral ideals, but they are worth pursuing in their own right. To subordinate all values to moral ones, to say that they must always yield to moral demands or at best can be "permissible" when morality allows it is to miss much of what makes life worth living for many of us. "A person," she concludes succinctly, "can be *perfectly wonderful* without being *perfectly moral*."[10]

Perhaps some of us would not want to go as far as Wolf does. They might say, for instance, that a boring world without hunger or disease is preferable to a richer world with them. This is not an unattractive view in many ways. However, even if we do so we must admit that Olympic swimmers and concert pianists continue to compel our appreciation. Even if we commit ourselves to the view that moral sainthood would be best for us, most of us cannot do so without a nagging sense that a world of moral saints would somehow be impoverished.[11]

The second type of normative complexity lies within the moral itself. It may be that human lives express conflicting moral values, that is, two or more values that both might be seen on the moral register but which come into conflict, or alternatively a value that appears morally admirable in some instances and not so much in others. It could be, for instance, that there are positive and negative consequences to an act and that those consequences resist any reduction to a common measure. Or that an intention can be morally conflicted or that certain ethical virtues are exclusive in such a way that to develop or express one requires suppressing another. The theories that dominate our thinking about morality can easily blind us to complex assessments within morality as well as between moral and other values.

It is important to be clear here. I am not saying that all of these moral theories themselves engage in forms of simplistic moral judgments about human lives. They do not. Strictly speaking, deontology and consequentialism don't speak directly of lives at all. Rather, they commend certain sorts of *actions*. Aristotle, by contrast, does speak of certain lives as better or—to be precise—happier or more flourishing than others, and commends those lives to us. Moreover, because of his doctrine of the unity of the virtues—the idea that the virtues are mutually supporting—his vision of a flourishing life is narrower than a vision that might see people as instantiating some virtues at the expense of others. On the other hand, Aristotle's virtues are more wide ranging than the criteria for good action prescribed by either consequentialism or deontology.

What unites these theories is their privileging of certain values, values that we have called moral or ethical, above all others and placing them at the center of our normative assessment. This may tempt us to take a narrower, more reductionist view of human beings when judging them on their character or trajectory. Regardless of which view we embrace, if we use it as the sole lens to assess a human life we will miss the complexity that many—indeed most—lives involve. In order to recognize this, however, it is not enough just to say it. Instead, displaying the normative complexity of specific human lives, inviting us to view them through a more supple normative lens, or even several lenses, is likely to get us to appreciate a fact that when granted at the abstract level might easily, under the sway of our traditional moral thinking, give way to more reductionist judgments. Lonergan's films, because they display precisely this complexity, are well situated to allow us access to these lenses.

Immaturity and Spontaneity

We have seen several aspects of Terry Prescott's life. He has been damaged by his parents' deaths in ways that leave him less capable of confronting adult challenges than the many others of us. We don't know how this happened, since we do not see the intervening years between that death and his current life. But we do see the effects. He wanders from place to place, unable to commit to relationships or other life projects, with the important exception of his commitment—however ambivalent at moments—to his sister. It is hard to imagine him holding down a steady job, not simply because he is a free spirit but because he is a decidedly unfree one. He is not so much burdened by his life as carrying his burdens with him, allowing them to dominate him in ways that prohibit him from taking hold of himself and casting his life in one or another particular form.

Moreover, Terry deceives himself about all this. Rather than reflecting on his inability to commit to longer-term projects that will give his life a shape, he looks resentfully upon a world that seems the source of his problems. He fancies himself as a rebel against the (rightly perceived) provincial rigidity of Scottsville when he is in fact in thrall to the town by means of a rebellion he can neither complete nor abandon. He is not an alternative to the narrow mores of small-town life; rather, he is an inversion of them, bound to them by the very fact of that inversion.

In the voice-over to *Count*, Lonergan says of Terry that, "He's sad and angry, and people like that lash out." But then he goes on: "That's not all of who he is but that's part of who he is." Not all, but part. Once again we see Lonergan recognizing that one never meets a human being who is not a full human being. Terry is a full human being, sad and angry, immature and irresponsible, lost and self-deceptive in ways that undercut him, but that is not all. That's part of who he is. Moreover, some of who he is that is morally objectionable is inseparable from some of who he is that is attractive if not admirable, particularly in the circumstances in which he finds himself.

To see this more clearly, let's focus on a scene early in the relationship between Terry and Rudy. Sammy has been prohibited by her boss Brian from her standard practice of picking Rudy up when his school lets out and dropping him off at a friend's house. Since Terry is going to be staying for a while—now that his girlfriend has tried to commit suicide and her parents are refusing to allow Terry any contact with her—Sammy asks him to do the pickup and drop-off. Terry agrees. However, Sammy gets a call from her friend that Rudy has not arrived at the house. She leaves work and goes looking for Rudy (and Terry, although he is not her major concern at this point). She finds the two of them among a carpentry crew that is building the frame for a house.

In this scene, Terry is showing Rudy how to hammer a nail into the wood frame of the house more efficiently. Rudy had been grasping the hammer near the top, and so has little leverage in swinging the hammer. Terry shows him how to grasp the hammer at the bottom and drive the nail in with fewer strokes. After Terry leaves him to it, Rudy tries Terry's method, has difficulty aiming correctly at the nail, and then returns to his previous method.

The scene is shot from straight on, looking directly at Terry and Rudy. From this angle, it appears as a classic father and son encounter, with a bit of humor at the end when Rudy, unseen by Terry, goes back to his earlier grasp of the hammer. Lonergan makes it easy to get caught up in the encounter and forget that it is in part a product of Terry's irresponsibility in failing to drop Rudy off at the friend's. It would not have been difficult for Terry, if he were not going to deliver Rudy to the friend's, to let the family know that he was taking him for the afternoon. Instead, however, he simply takes Rudy with him without bothering to inform anyone of this.

And there is more. Why are they at the building site in the first place? Presumably it has nothing to do with an inherent desire to practice carpentry. Terry needs money and has somehow figured out that there is a house-building project he can join for the afternoon. So he is taking Rudy with him to a job for him to make some money without going through the minimal effort of informing anyone who might need to know this. The irresponsibility and rudeness are palpable here, and in case we miss it the first time through, later in the film Terry just forgets to pick up Rudy from school, leaving him to walk in the rain to Sammy's bank for a ride to the friend's. Terry's self-centeredness and self-concern are on full display here.

And yet it is difficult to see this as nothing more than Terry's lack of concern for others. He doesn't just take Rudy to the building site. He has an eye on him and tries to help him develop a simple skill. Rudy himself is open to this—at least for the moment—trying to learn what Terry has taught him. In this moment Terry is displayed as occupying the role of a father figure of the type that Rudy is missing—and that we will discover later is a role Rudy's biological father is incapable of occupying. Terry expresses a warmth toward Rudy that fills a lack Rudy had been experiencing, since he does not even know who his father is. In fact, we are keyed into this lack early in the film when, one evening, for a writing assignment from school Rudy tells his mother (after her prodding questioning) that he is writing a story about his father as a superhero.

Moreover, the qualities that Terry displays in this scene are ones we can't help being drawn to, even to the point of forgetting for an instant that they are also the product of Terry's irresponsibility. First, Terry likes Rudy. Although, as we have discussed, this liking is not always paternal—rather it is often at a peer level—nevertheless he feels genuine regard for Rudy. His attempt to help Rudy does not come from any disinterested sense of duty toward him. It is difficult to see Terry as being moved by a disinterested sense of duty in any arena of his life. Rather, it comes from a motive that perhaps is the only motive that can move Terry to display caring toward others: he is fond of Rudy. From Rudy's perspective, though, this is probably the best motive that could move Terry. What's missing from Rudy's life is not someone with a sense of moral duty; it is someone, and better a male adult, who takes an interest in him, who likes him.

This liking comes out again, and again within the context of self-concern, in the scene at the bar we have already mentioned. Asked to babysit Rudy when she goes out on a date with Bob, Terry takes Rudy to a bar and bets on a game of pool that he plays, partnered up with Rudy. This, of course, is to be kept a secret from Sammy. In the game, Terry fails to win on his first turn, leaving only the eight ball unpocketed. His opponent also fails to clear the table, and so Rudy, who has no pool skills, must sink the eight ball to win the game. Terry works closely with him to tap the ball with the cue in the right way—a moment both tense and amusing. ("Don't even hit it. Just kiss it," he tells Rudy, who has no idea what he means.) When Rudy sinks the ball, Terry lifts him off the ground as the crowd cheers. Terry is clearly relieved, but also happy for Rudy, close to him in a way that is warm and at the same time a bit self-absorbed.

For Rudy, these moments of bonding are particularly important. They offer him a type of father–son or at least older brother–younger brother bond that he could not experience with Sammy, however solicitous she is of him. While they are in keeping with Terry's self-absorption—and in both cases involve his making money—they are inseparable from a real liking of Rudy that Terry has, a liking that Rudy can feel. In fact, later in the film when Sammy asks Terry to leave after the debacle with Rudy's biological father, Rudy asks Terry to take him along when he goes.

These moments do not fit the traditional model of moral action commended by virtue ethicists, deontologists, or utilitarians. Terry does not show a particular nobility of character in any of them, and he has no thought for what his moral duty would be nor whether he is choosing to cause the most good. He has brought Rudy along to activities he would like to be doing anyway; the bond developed between them arises in that context. Does this mean that his actions should not be described as moral but rather as something else?

Recently another way of thinking about ethics has arisen that at first glance might offer a path to considering Terry's actions within a moral framework. What has come to be called "care ethics," grounded in feminist theory, criticizes the intellectualist bent of traditional moral theories and focuses instead on the moral aspects of emotional relationships between and among people. One philosopher who articulates an ethics of care, Virginia Held, notes that we are always in relationship to one another. The recognition of this is often lost on more traditional moral theories. It is as though these theories are in danger of treating each of us as an individual on their own, without relation, who then comes to others equipped with a set of moral principles, which are subsequently applied to those others in our behavior. But we aren't like that. We are always already involved with many other people, navigating the world alongside and with them. According to Held, any adequate moral view needs to reflect this fact. As she insists, "our embeddedness in familial, social, and historical contexts is basic."[12]

To see ourselves as individuals divorced from our social contexts, forming principles that are then applied to those contexts through our behavior, is, for philosophers like Held, to take things the wrong way around. This is not to say that there is no place for moral principles. Rather, it is to say that our ethics ought to arise first and foremost out of a recognition that those whom our behavior affects are not only other people surrounding us but more deeply people with whom we are already in various kinds of relationships, and moreover, although this is not a central concern for us here, that those relationships already help constitute who we are.

However, even an ethics of care would not capture exactly what is happening between Terry and Rudy. Terry's motives, while allowing him to bond with Rudy, are always a bit compromised by his own self-absorption. By "compromised" here I don't mean that there is anything immoral about them. That would be a claim too rooted in traditional moral theory. Rather, the care that he shows toward Rudy is limited by his inability to get very far outside himself, to recognize the effects of his behavior on Rudy. This limitation comes out several times in the film in the form of displays of immaturity, as we have seen. When he mistakenly thinks that Rudy has told Sammy about their evening at the bar or even when he is confronted by the pastor, Terry takes out his frustrations on Rudy in ways that are hurtful to him without Terry's showing any real recognition of this.[13]

And yet there is care going on as well, a bond that, limited as it is, gets established between them. It's a bond Terry fosters and it is grounded not only in his self-absorption but also in a genuine liking of Rudy. While a care ethics would not entirely capture what is going on between them, it would not be entirely beside the point either.

We might put this—as long as we don't give it too utilitarian an interpretation—by saying that Terry's alloyed caring for Rudy creates a bond that results in some real good coming into Rudy's life. There is something going on here that moral theories seek to capture, but not precisely in the way they seek to capture it.

There is another aspect to Terry's behavior, one that displays a value, what can be called a "narrative value," that we have seen before but should return to in this context. Terry has a spontaneity that comes out in these scenes that, while not really a moral characteristic, can draw us to him—and sometimes away from him. We can see it in the scenes described above. When Terry takes Rudy along with him to earn some money at carpentry or to play pool, it is not likely with a lot of forethought about these engagements or their consequences. More or less, in Terry's thinking, it seems like a good idea at the time. His spontaneity comes out, however, not only in his decisions about what to do but also in his emotional reactions. His hugging Rudy after Rudy sinks the shot is an involuntary emotional display that would be more difficult for Sammy to express, partially because she's so concerned about what would be good for Rudy. To be sure, there is Terry's relief at having won money rather than lost it. But there is also a warmth toward Rudy at that moment that comes out unfiltered in his hug.

It is in part this spontaneity that infects Sammy, giving her a sense of permission to break the norms of the town—norms that have bound her for years—by having an affair with her boss. It is also this spontaneity that creates one of the lightest moments in the film, when she confides her affair to Terry as they stand on the porch of her house one evening. Laura Linney plays the moment of Sammy's confession of the affair with a striking combination of guilt and carefreeness, laughing and leaning in to Terry as her voice expresses the recognition of the wrongness of her action. She tells Terry what she has done not simply because he is her brother. Not any brother with any personality will do. Rather, she tells him because he is *Terry*, her brother in whom she can confide her transgressions because he will not moralize to her in the way most folks in the town would. And this is not only because he rejects the town's morality but also because it is a spontaneity to which he can relate.

This does not require that we, as viewers, need to approve morally of Sammy's affair. That is precisely the point. At this moment in the film, we—or at least I—feel ambivalent. On the one hand, it is hard to approve of someone's having an affair with a man whose wife is pregnant and clearly unhappy. On the other hand, given the difficulty of Sammy's life as a single mother with an entirely absent father in a small town, her joy in breaking the rules is difficult entirely to condemn. There is something about it—and, to be sure, about the way Laura Linney plays it—that draws, if not admiration, then at least emotional resonance. Her joy is infectious.

The ambivalence we feel here is a clue that we are in the presence of two very different types of values, a moral value and what I am calling a narrative value. I have discussed the possible conflicts of these two types of values elsewhere and won't expand on that here.[14] What should be recognized at the moment is that people's lives express not only moral values but other kinds of values as well. In looking at their lives, it is worth keeping in mind these other values so as not to place an entirely moralistic assessment on who they are.

However, and on the other hand, there are times when only moral assessment will do, when the nonmoral value that is expressed is just better off being left unexpressed. We see this in the case of Terry's bringing Rudy to see his biological father. This, too, is a spontaneous decision that arises as the two of them are fishing. The father's rejection of Rudy, if not the subsequent fight between the father and Terry, is, in retrospect for the viewer but certainly in prospect for Terry, entirely predictable. There is a good reason Sammy has kept Rudy from his father: his father wants nothing to do with him. Terry undoubtedly knows this and yet gets the impulse that Rudy should meet his father and, without considering the consequences, acts on that impulse. It should never have happened and, among other things, it results in Sammy's asking Terry to stop staying at her house.

The relationship between nonmoral values like spontaneity and moral ones, as well as the relationship among various moral values, is a complicated one. It is complicated not only in abstract philosophical terms but also in its expression in the particularities of a human life. Terry's life displays a normative complexity that evades simple judgment or assessment. If we turn to the life of Lee Chandler, we can see this complexity from another angle, one more strictly tied up with morality than with nonmoral values. His life is, among other things, an intricate study of moral permission, or better forgiveness and condemnation, one that even challenges us to make clear the distinction between the two.

Comprehension and Condemnation

Say you're sitting at a bar near closing time. You watch someone cross over from one side of the bar to the other and pick a fight with the patrons on the other side. Those patrons weren't looking for a fight. They were enjoying their drinks, having a friendly conversation, perhaps avoiding the prospect of having to go home only to get up and soldier off to work the next day. They see this stranger approach them and, while one of them tries to calm the man's obvious belligerence, the other is more confrontative, insisting the stranger has no business bothering them. Suddenly this man lashes out, punching not only the more confrontative one in the face but also his more reluctant companion.

Or suppose you're sitting in a different bar. You see a man brush up against another man as he's heading to the bathroom. Out of nowhere, the other man punches him, again in the face, and has to be restrained by five or six other people to stop beating him and striking out at everyone who comes near him. There was no provocation; it looks as though this other man was just looking for a fight.

How do you react? What do you think? Well, first, if you're sitting at one of these bars you're probably going to react with some mix of fear and anger. The man who started these fights is powerful and seems as likely to hurt you as he did one of the other patrons. It's just luck he didn't go up to your table or you didn't brush against him on the way to the bathroom. That is the frightening part. But there's also an injustice involved. After all, these people didn't come to the bar for a fight and they certainly didn't come to the bar to get hurt. They came to enjoy themselves, some of them in the company of their friends. And yet here comes this individual with a chip on his shoulder looking to take out his own problems on some other innocent people, attacking them almost at random.

You would probably judge this person harshly. Who does this sort of thing? What kind of a jerk—or worse—punches people in the face for no reason? Perhaps, in the moment, you might ask whether the world would even be better off without him.

It is an understandable reaction. We are moral judges of what we ourselves witness, of what comes before us. (And, as we will see in a moment, we are often moral judges of what we hear second hand.) How could it be otherwise? And yet, let's recognize what we are doing here. There is not one judgment here, but two. The second one follows the first one and is based on it. The first judgment is of the act, of what the person did. It was a correct judgment. The act—both acts in this case—was wrong. Assaulting people without provocation is morally indecent. One doesn't need a moral theory for that.

The second judgment, the more problematic one, is of the person on the basis of the act. The question of what kind of a jerk would do this is grounded in the observation of a single act (or maybe two, if one spends a lot of time in bars between Boston and Manchester). We know of this person only what we have seen of him, and come to our assessment of him based on that. What else do we have?

If we did this, we would not be alone. Many of the people in *Manchester by the Sea* did the same thing. Lonergan himself, in a cameo appearance in the film, did it. After Lee and Patrick leave the attorney's office where Lee has just found out that Joe has designated Lee as Patrick's guardian, they get into a disagreement about whether Patrick can keep Joe's boat. Lee, in his frustration, says, "Patty, I swear to God, I'm gonna knock your fuckin' block off." At that moment Lonergan, dressed in professional wear, walks by. He briefly turns back and says, "Great parenting." It is a moment of snap judgment, one that, we know, is not only technically wrong since Lee is Patrick's uncle, but also an inaccurate summation of a long, sometimes complicated, but certainly deep relationship between the two of them. And yet, were we the ones walking by, we might have said (or at least thought) the same thing.

In Manchester, of course, this is not the only judgment Lee faces on the basis of a single act. During the short period he tries to commit to living in Manchester—the period after Joe's death and before he meets Randy on the street—he tries to get a job there. As we have seen, after his first attempt the manager tells the person he talked with that she doesn't want to see him there again. In the following scenes we see Lee from a distance talking with other people, clearly seeking a job. There is no dialogue in these scenes, only music, and they are shot from a distance. However, we know what is going on. He is not going to get a job in Manchester. He is not just Lee Chandler; he is THE Lee Chandler, the man who negligently killed his children and then left town.

In fact, because the fire scene is shown in the film after Lee arrives back in Manchester to pick up Patrick from school after Joe's death, we learn of Lee's infamy before we know what he is infamous for. In fact, we learn it twice. First, when he calls the vice principal of Patrick's school to inform him of Joe's death, the assistant sitting with the vice principal, upon learning who is on the phone, asks incredulously, "*Lee Chandler?*" to which the vice principal responds, "The very one." Second, a few minutes later, when he appears at Patrick's ice hockey practice the coach says, after learning who he is, "That's Lee Chandler? *The* Lee Chandler?" We understand that he has done something terrible or at least is associated with some sort of tragedy, but we don't yet know what it is.

We never learn the exact character of Lee's reputation in Manchester. Like the gap in *Count*, where we don't learn about the lives of Terry and

Sammy Prescott during the period between their parents' death and the film's present except through hints offered in their conversation, we never see the period between the fire and Lee's return to Manchester. With characteristic economy, Lonergan presents us only with a few gestures and allows us to fill in the rest with our imagination. What is clear, however, is that the general sentiment of the town is that Lee has done something unforgivable and is no longer welcome. He is no longer one of them. To put it in philosophical terms, he is no longer a member of their moral community.

In this sense, we are more privileged epistemically than most of the people of *Manchester by the Sea* (with the exception of friends like George), and because of this we cannot come to the same judgment as they. For them, he is defined by a single moment. But the film's audience sees two things that are not available to most of the townspeople. First, we see Lee in his life before the fire. He is close to his family, and especially to his kids. We see his warmth and playfulness with them as well as with Patrick. In the opening scene on the boat with Patrick and Joe, years before the fire, he displays a paternal regard for Patrick as well as an easy-going manner. (Later in the film, when Lee comes out of himself at moments, it is because of Patrick's influence and the history of their relationship.) It is not by accident, then, that the person who is displayed during much of the film as unable to do more than soldier through his days is given charge of Joe's son when Joe dies (recalling that Patrick's mother is, for all Joe knows, entirely out of the picture).

As important as these moments in Lee's prefire life are, the fire scene itself refuses to allow us to come to the same moral judgment of Lee as much of the town does. To be sure, many people in the town are there.

When Lee sees the fire, he must walk through a crowd of people to get near his house. However, they are anonymous to us. Moreover, they do not witness up close Lee's reaction; they don't have our intimacy with him during those devastating hours. In her profile of Lonergan, Rebecca Mead discusses a detail of the fire scene. In the scene, Lee keeps holding on to the bag of groceries he has carried back with him from the store. He doesn't drop them or toss them in a majestic gesture of pain. He just clutches them. Casey Affleck describes it this way: "That was written into the script—that he is holding this bag. It is one of the few scenes where, when I read it, I thought, What is going on here? ... if I have to get upset, I can get myself to feeling upset. But why does he want me holding a bag? Then, when we came to do the scene, it made perfect sense. The character—he doesn't scream and gnash his teeth and pull out his hair. He is just clamped down on himself ... He is just trying to hold on, and that ends up carrying over into so much more."[15]

What we, the audience, experience at that moment is not a man who has caused the death of his children. We don't even learn about the fire screen until later. Instead, we experience a man in the throes of nearly unimaginable grief, a man watching his world fall apart. And to underline the point, Lee is still standing there when one of the firemen carries out a small body bag that clearly contains one of his children. After this, it is impossible to relate to Lee as the official narrative of the town would have him. To be sure, it is not impossible to see his negligence. What is impossible is to reduce him to it.

So what do we make of the person who twice attacked innocent folks at a bar, in one case seeming to break the nose of someone who was trying to de-escalate the situation? We needn't excuse it. There is no reason for that. The act was wrong, morally wrong on any accounting. And we can't, as we could with Terry Prescott, recognize other values in play, values that might be expressed in more worthwhile ways in other situations. And yet we cannot morally dismiss Lee Chandler either. He is not simply THE Lee Chandler that the townspeople see. He is also a tragic figure that, through a negligence he would undoubtedly have given his own life to undo, bears a guilt that would shatter us just as surely as it has shattered him.

Jean-Paul Sartre once said, "There is no reality except in action … Man is nothing else than his plan; he exists only to the extent that he fulfills himself; he is therefore nothing else than the ensemble of his acts, nothing else than his life."[16] We need to be careful if we are to endorse this view. If Lee is nothing other than his acts, then he is, perhaps with the exception of his relationship with Patrick, to be morally condemned, or at least disapproved of. He may not be condemned for the fire, which was accidental and unintentional. And he may get cut some moral slack for helping Patrick. But viewed entirely from the perspective of outward behavior, there is little morally to endorse in Lee after the fire. Perhaps, then, we should view him more widely. What one does may properly be the subject of moral praise or condemnation. But what holds for actions may not hold for people's lives. Lee is not only what he does but also what he has undergone. He is his violence, but he is also his grief. He is his incessant moodiness, but he is also his struggle to get through the day. The complications of his life, and not just his actions, are moral, and in putting him to judgment we need to recognize those complications and recognize that they too are moral—or at least morally relevant.

It is a lesson we would all do well to apply in our own lives, difficult as it may be. In particular, it is always tempting to condemn others on the basis of what we see them do. This holds especially for strangers or people we do not know well. And, on the one hand, there is behavior, even everyday behavior, that it is right to judge morally, even where it may not be right to intervene. (The question of intervention is a separate one.) When a father slaps his child across the face at the playground, when a work colleague bullies another, when a student cheats on an exam, when someone makes a racist or homophobic remark, these are not to be excused. And they are not always the sideways expression of a hidden grief or wound. There are bad parents, people who just enjoy bullying, others who cheat just to get ahead, and still others whose racism or homophobia is a central expression of who they are. But not always. And in many cases we do not know who the person behaving badly is or what their life has been like. Among those we don't know well, we often cannot tell what they have undergone to lead to this behavior we properly condemn. We do not know whether we are witnessing a Donald Trump or a Lee Chandler.

It is difficult to navigate our lives with this moral uncertainty in mind. And yet, among the lessons *Manchester* has to teach us is precisely this one: there is moral complexity of which we may not be aware. The difference between what we in the audience know about Lee Chandler and what most of the townspeople know illustrates this. Inasmuch as Lee's grief counts as morally relevant in an assessment of his character, so we must recognize that there are hidden griefs and struggles others engage in that may be relevant to our judgment of them. Not always, but sometimes, even often. Because those griefs and struggles are hidden it is often unclear how to form moral judgment. And it is precisely that lack of clarity we must learn to accept.

Navigating Moral Complexity

Let's return to the scene in *Margaret* where Lisa shows up to Maretti's house to confront him about the accident. It is a scene that can be read within a simple moral frame. In that scene, Lisa is talking deontologically while Maretti is talking consequentially. For Lisa, the issue is that there is guilt involved and it must be addressed. What she wants from her conversation with Maretti is not entirely clear, but it involves an acknowledgment between them that they caused the death of Monica Patterson. In the unfolding of film, Lisa doesn't go after Maretti with Emily and the attorney until *after* this conversation. What she seems to want here is an acknowledgment, one that will not necessarily have any particular consequences, that they participated in causing someone to die. In the conversation, after Maretti tells her the consequences of any public acknowledgment of what she actually saw (the light turning red), she says, "I just want to say what really happened," insisting twice, "It was both our fault."

Maretti, for his part, is not going to participate in this. He seems to think that what Lisa wants is to recant her earlier story in front of the police and then implicate both of them in Monica's death. Although she does not say this, neither does she deny it. Lisa seems at this moment to want to assuage her own guilt and perhaps feels she can do it if the two of them come to an agreement about what really happened. She seems to feel that the two of them have some kind of tacit communication between them, one that goes back to the accident itself. In her conversation with Maretti, she says that when they were being interviewed by the police, "it seemed like you were kind of looking at me—like we were saying to each other, 'Let's not say anything about what happened.'"

Maretti, however, is having none of this. He denies that there was any communication and is concerned solely with the consequences of what any acknowledgment of the events might bring.

> You wanna ruin my life, start telling 'em [i.e. the police] about looks, and you waved at me and I had my cowboy hat, go ahead! You're going to go back to school and do your homework and I'm going to lose my job! And who's going to feed my kids? You? Are you gonna do it? And for what? She's dead! She's dead! And there's nothin' I can do to bring her back!

It is an entirely consequentialist speech. There is nothing that confessing the truth of the events (a truth whose possibility he denies—when the light turned red he was looking at Lisa and so could not have known whether it was red or green) will make anything better. To speak entirely philosophically, the sum total of utility of any acknowledgment will be outweighed by the sum total of disutility.

For those versed in the classic traditions of moral philosophy, this is an exemplary case of contrasting moral views crossing paths without touching. What is morally salient for the deontologist, among other things, is the proper allocation of guilt and innocence and the willingness to acknowledge honestly what one has done. For the consequentialist, the issue has to do with the results of one's actions, not the intentions behind them. Lisa and Maretti are not going to come to an agreement about what happened because, among other things, they are starting from two different moral places. (Of course there is more going on here as well, among which is Maretti's worry that Lisa means for any shared acknowledgment of guilt to become public.) I am not saying that that is what Lonergan sought to do—stage a conflict between a deontological and a consequentialist view. I think it's pretty unlikely that he was interested in contrasting deontology and consequentialism. Rather, that's just what happened, and it is illustrative of the ways deontologists and consequentialists find themselves talking past each other.

We have just now used the terms *deontologist* and *consequentialist* as adjectives to describe people rather than positions. In academic philosophy that might be an appropriate application to certain people. However, when it is appropriate, it is in reference to their philosophical positions, not their lives. A deontologist in academic philosophy is someone who philosophically endorses a view that finds the moral salience of actions in their intentions or more broadly their means rather than their outcomes or ends, and vice versa for the consequentialist. It may, if the philosopher seeks to apply her philosophical position to her life, also accurately characterize the way she tries to live, and more or less the way she does live. But for most of us, our moral lives are more complicated than that. We may think and act deontologically at some moments and consequentially at others—and in still other ways at other moments. Whether we can consistently bring those moments together into a larger moral picture is often uncertain, and rarely attempted, even among many dedicated moral philosophers.

Such moral consistency is certainly not a concern of Lisa's, which makes her in this way more like the rest of us than like the moral philosopher who strives for philosophical consistency—at least in theory. (It is difficult to say more about Maretti, since we see so little of him in the film and nothing—except one quick shot late in the movie while he's driving a bus that passes Lisa and her mother Joan—after their conversation.) In the wake of her experience with Maretti Lisa takes a more consequentialist stance toward him. Rather than showing concern for his duty and hers, she believes that he should be punished in good part to prevent him from causing further harm. For instance, in her first conversation with both Emily and Emily's friend who is an attorney, at one point Lisa say that "the whole point is to get this guy ..." at which point Emily interrupts, misunderstanding where Lisa is headed, to say, "Is to fucking *get* this guy," at which point Lisa corrects her: "No, it's to get him out from behind the wheel of a bus!" It is the further effects of his actions rather than his duty to admit what he has helped cause, which Lisa recognizes is not going to happen, that are now of moral concern to her.

One might want to question here whether in fact Lisa's judgment has left the deontological and become consequentialist. After all, a deontologist can endorse punishment. Broadly, that would occur when a person *deserves* punishment. Punishment is a matter of desert rather than consequences. So couldn't we see Lisa as still operating within a consistent deontological moral framework regarding the accident?

Things are actually quite complicated here, in part because of the issue of self-deception discussed in the previous chapter. In her public moral stance, after her discussion with Maretti, Lisa takes a largely consequentialist stance toward him. He needs to be removed from his position in order to prevent further harm to others. Recall that for Lisa the settlement from the bus company is not important; what's important is that he not be allowed to place others in danger.

However, one might see—rightfully in my view—a bit of vengeance at work as well. Maretti has not admitted his guilt to Lisa, which places her in a position where she confronts the possibility that only she will admit guilt—at least to herself. The possibility of a cooperative recognition of guilt is lost when Maretti refuses to recognize his role in the accident—that he might have run a red light when Lisa was talking with him. Moreover, his refusal rings hollow. During their conversation, at one point he tries to account for his behavior by saying, "Maybe I was wavin' at you, like wavin' to say, you know, 'Step away from the bus,' if the bus was in motion I would have waved you away for your own safety, but that's all that would be." Given the events we have seen on the screen, it would be unlikely that Maretti would have thought that was a real possibility.

Mixed in with a consequentialist view of punishment, then, might be a desire for vengeance. This would place it closer in structure to a deontological view, since it would make the punishment more a matter of what Lisa thought Maretti deserved rather than the consequences of punishing him. But we must be careful here. The desire for vengeance is not the same thing as the recognition that someone deserves punishment, although it might feel that way to someone with that desire. And the reason Lisa might have that desire in the first place is her anger and fear in the wake of Maretti's refusal to recognize his role in Monica Patterson's death. And so we seem to have something like the following: Lisa's guilt over what has happened is increased by the fact that she is now alone with it; that also makes her angry with Maretti; that anger leads to a desire for vengeance; that desire is at least structurally close to the recognition of desert; therefore pressing a deontological case for punishment might lead back to a recognition of a desire for vengeance; thus the safest moral option (prompted by a degree of self-deception) is to take a consequentialist position—Maretti should be removed from his position for reasons of public safety.

This is all a bit speculative, but is in keeping both with the previous discussion of self-deception and with Lonergan's broadly psychoanalytic orientation. It also displays how psychological and moral themes can be woven together in ways that, among other things, complicate the moral positions a person takes. We should not read this, however, as saying that Lisa's consequentialism is nothing more than a cover for her psychological guilt. The consequentialist issues she raises with Maretti are real ones; moreover, they are lent more substance when we are confronted with Maretti's flimsy excuses for why he was waving his hat at Lisa. A person who so cavalierly dismisses the possibility of his own negligent behavior may indeed be a risky bet to drive a bus. And, in fact, Emily's attorney friend later discovers that Maretti has had two previous accidents, but because his brother-in-law is an influential member of the Transit Workers Union, they were not followed up on.

In the end, however, Lisa's consequentialist case does not get a hearing. The bus company settles with Abigail but without any admission of guilt. Not only Lisa, but also many of us may feel that justice was not done in this case, and in that way may be sympathetic to Lisa's frustration.[17]

We have focused so far only on one aspect of Lisa's moral life, her relationship to Maretti in regard to the events surrounding the accident. To be sure, the accident is the central moment of the film, but *Margaret* makes clear that it is not the only aspect of Lisa Cohen's life. Her life, and her moral life, is reducible neither to the event of Monica Patterson's death nor to her ongoing reaction to the events to which it gives rise. Lisa is also an adolescent at school, struggling in math and with a crush on her math teacher, Mr. Aaron (Matt Damon)—a crush that eventuates in her seducing him, to his immediate regret. She is also a daughter of divorced parents, seeking the approval of one and in a close but volatile relationship with the other. She is someone discovering her sexuality, a discovery that leads to her losing her virginity and eventually to an abortion. She is also a friend to her classmate Darren (John Gallagher, Jr.) who has a crush on her that she does not reciprocate and is trying to steer through. In all these areas she is seeking to navigate her way through a world that, as the movie makes clear not only in the intricacies of the accident and subsequent investigation and lawsuit but throughout the film, is much larger than she is. (At one point in the film we see Lisa from the back walking through a crowded street in what appears to be midtown Manhattan, eventually blending into the sea of people around her.)

In all these arenas she is learning to handle—or refusing to learn to handle—the moral demands that are placed upon her. She does so not through adopting a moral theory but instead by confronting the situations as they arise for her. For instance, her relationship with her mother, Joan, who is not only an actress but also a bit of a drama queen in her outside life, is displayed not only through loud and at times abusive verbal confrontations (an adolescent engaged with an adult drama queen is rarely a pretty sight) but also through an underlying closeness that emerges in the final shot of the film where the two are sitting together at the opera weeping together. If we were to give a moral description of it, it would be less in terms of consequentialism or deontology but instead more in terms of the care ethics we noted above in the section on Terry Prescott. And even so, given the periodically explosive nature of their interactions, a simple explanation in terms of care ethics would not entirely capture that relationship either.

We might say that Lisa, like most of us, is trying to make her way through a world where understanding is often elusive, people's motivations (including one's own) are complicated and at times contradictory, and resolution is often hard to come by. As we saw, for Lonergan, "You can just see the framework a little better with a teen-ager. Grownups are more settled into who they are going to be and what their place in the world is. Teen-agers are kind of poking around and trying different ways of being, ways of acting." It is not that adults are not navigating the same kinds of issues that adolescents are. Rather, they carve themselves a path that keeps them at bay—unless, like Lee Chandler, something happens that prevents them from doing so.

So is moral theory completely irrelevant to the way most of us live? That would be saying far too much. We may not often (or ever) apply Kant's Categorical Imperative to our actions, but do we often seek to treat people as worthy of a basic level of respect? We may not calculate consequences, but we often ask which of our actions will make things better than other choices that we might make. And we mostly do not seek to cultivate particular Aristotelian virtues, but we periodically reflect on what kinds of people we are, particularly when confronted with personal shortcomings. Our moral lives, like our broader normative lives and our lives more generally, are complicated affairs, affairs that resist easy categorization or consistent moral approaches, but that may be enhanced through more rigorous reflection on who we are and what we are doing.

Projects and Values

The philosopher Bernard Williams, in a critique of what he thinks of as the sterility of modern moral philosophy, points out that people's lives are deeply entwined with what he calls their *projects*. He says, "an individual person has a set of desires, concerns, or, as I shall often call them, projects, which help constitute a *character*."[18] He further clarifies this by saying that, "one's pattern of interests, desires, and projects not only provide the reason for an interest in what happens within the horizon of one's future, but also constitute the conditions of there being such a future at all."[19] We can unpack the idea this way. People are not simply a set of unconnected acts. Our lives unfold in temporal trajectories, which are characterized by engagements that are more or less central to those lives. Some of those engagements, which Williams calls "categorical desires," are central to us. It is hard to imagine us going on, or at least going on as *us*, without them. Other projects and desires are less central, but nevertheless their "pattern" establishes our character, who we are.

Although Williams does not say so, some of these projects can be self-deceptive. As we have seen in the previous chapter, there can be ways of engaging the world that are part of who someone is but that one would be loathe to admit, even to oneself. Otherwise put, there are projects people have that do not accord with what they would reflectively endorse as their values, aspects of themselves that reveal things they indeed treat as valuable but would reject as values if asked whether they indeed endorsed them. Terry Prescott's ongoing rebellion and Lisa's futile project of obtaining her father's affection are examples of these.

With Williams, as with Sartre, we should be careful in our understanding of projects. Just as with Lee Chandler, whose life consists not only in what he does but also in what he has undergone, we need to be expansive in understanding the relationship between a person's projects and her life. Otherwise it becomes too easy to pass negative (or perhaps sometimes positive) moral judgment on someone without an adequate comprehension of who they are—an ease that most of us engage in all too often. Indeed, part of Williams's own goal in positing the idea of projects is to wrest our thought about people from the moral reductionism to acts that he thinks is characteristic of modern moral philosophy, to remove us from the idea that morality "requires abstraction from particular circumstances and particular characteristics of the parties, including the agent, except in so far as these can be treated as universal features of any morally similar situation."[20]

If we begin to think of lives as unfolding over a temporal trajectory rather than in a series of discrete acts, and as involved in engagements of various kinds in that trajectory—some of which we can admit to ourselves and others not so much—then we can begin to see that the richness of lives escapes an accounting that would reduce them to a moral assessment of individual acts. Further, we can see this in at least two ways, one moral and one nonmoral.

On the moral side, we can see, as with Terry Prescott's spontaneity, that certain engagements in the world can sometimes have morally positive effects and sometimes not, depending on the situation. Terry's expression of joy when Rudy sinks the eight ball as well as his loosening of the grip of the town's rigidity on his sister are manifestations of that spontaneity and its effects, but so is his destructive decision to take Rudy to see his biological father. If we judge these acts independent of one another, as an utilitarian might, we may perhaps capture the moral status of each act adequately enough, but Terry himself goes missing. (If, by contrast, we take a Kantian view of these acts, none of them are to be morally approved of since none of them arise from a sense of moral duty.) In order to see him more fully, we need to step away from the acts and see them as an expression of who he is, of his being, and of his engagements.

It might seem that, in this case, an Aristotelian view would be more adequate to the case. In his writings, Williams himself sometimes leans in that direction.[21] However, if we think of virtues in more strictly moral terms we will continue to miss the richness of Lonergan's characters, as well as the richness of many people around us. Spontaneity, as well as values like intensity, adventurousness, spirituality, steadfastness, and others are difficult to incorporate into a moral picture of the world, although they may be qualities of character that we admire in others or aspire to ourselves. While an Aristotelian approach removes ethical judgment from acts and places it on qualities of character, inasmuch as it provides a moral answer to the question of how one should live—or even seeks a unitary answer to that question—it will neglect ways of living, themes of a life, that while not providing a moral example will still strike many of us as nevertheless worthwhile.

In a striking essay entitled "Good-for-Nothings," Susan Wolf, whose critique of moral saintliness we have already seen, argues that if we assess the contributions of most of us to the fields we find ourselves in, we'll find that they don't amount to much. Philosophy, for instance, would get along just fine if almost any philosopher, living or dead, had decided to do something else. There are very few philosophers whose work shapes the field to such an important extent that their absence would be a deep loss for the philosophical endeavor. And what goes for philosophy goes for most other areas as well. The vast majority of artists, scientists, athletes, actors, writers, and others will not contribute anything to their fields that would be missed should they have chosen their lives differently.

Even if this is true, however, Wolf argues that it doesn't imply what it might seem to at first glance. We should not go to the other extreme of saying that there is no point to our participation in these activities. Instead of asking how much good each of us brings to the field we participate in, we should recognize the goodness of the field itself as a reason to participate in it. "If we understand the world as containing objects and opportunities for experience that are of value in themselves, then we may think of our lives as better, more fortunate, insofar as we are able to be in appreciative touch with some of the most valuable of these." A little further on she continues, "The world seems full of things of immeasurable value, including objects and environments of the natural world, works of supreme human accomplishment, not to mention people themselves, and it is a kind of good fortune to be able to interact with these, in a way that involves going some way toward understanding and appreciating their value."[22]

I believe that Wolf is making a deep point here, but one that we must be careful about in applying to people rather than, as she does, to opportunities for participation. As she argues, in addition to moral goodness there are many other kinds of goodness in the world. Those other kinds of goodness are given their worth not simply because they are instrumental in making our lives better in some other ways, but rather because they are worth participating in in themselves. Let's apply this to people, though. Terry Prescott is, among other things, spontaneous. I think we can say that it is good that there is spontaneity in the world, that humans—or at least some of us—are built in such a way as to be able to participate in spontaneity. This is also true for adventurousness, spirituality, intensity, and other values. In short, there are a number of values that we would not call moral ones that it is good we have access to, that "it is good fortune to interact with."

However, since we are talking about people rather than fields of endeavor, it is also true that the expression of these nonmoral values in people's behavior can in fact be good for others, specific others. And the fact that it is specific others is important here. Wolf does not argue that, for instance, the paintings of Dutch Master Gerrit Dou did not bring pleasure or aesthetic enhancement to anyone's life. He painted, people saw his paintings, and that was good for them. Rather, her argument is that, "there were so many Dutch Masters in the seventeenth century that it is at least arguable that the artworld did not need every single one of them to supply its patrons ... It is not obvious therefore that had Gerrit Dou, say, become a chemist instead of a painter, it would have been worse *for* anyone."[23] People who did not have the chance to encounter Dou's work would not have missed the artistic experience associated with the Dutch Masters, because they would have had plenty of others to choose from.

This is not the case with people. Had Terry Prescott not been born, and had Sammy's parents still been killed, she would very likely have had things go worse for her than they actually did. Having a brother helped her cope with her life after her parents' death. While in one sense it is true that she would not have suffered a loss had he not been born—in order for there to be a loss he would have had to be there in the first place—it is also true that her life would have been impoverished relative to the life she in fact had with him. Moreover, we can be specific about what it is about Terry that enriches Sammy's life. Terry's spontaneity itself, although maddening and sometimes destructive, also enhances her world. It does not necessarily make her morally better. Indeed, it may have encouraged her or at least offered her some kind of permission to have an affair with her boss. But it did open her to aspects of herself that had gotten buried over the years, aspects that at least granted her a moral holiday from the constrained life she was leading most of the time in the small town of Scottsville.

We should be clear here. I am not arguing that Terry Prescott is a model of nonmoral values, any more than that we should excuse everything Lee Chandler did or dismiss Lisa Cohen's self-deceptions as mere adolescent foibles. Rather, the idea is that the field of values is normatively complex. It is complex, as we have just seen, in Lisa Cohen's life. But it is also complex in the interaction between moral and nonmoral values. In fact, although it would take us too far afield to address this adequately, it might be suggested that this complexity renders it difficult to tell where the field of moral values ends and the arena—or arenas—of nonmoral values begins. Fortunately, we do not need to address that question here. Rather, our concern is with people more than with fields of values. And in regard to people, we have seen that, among the things that Lonergan's films show us, any assessment or judgment we are to come of them requires an engagement with more than their behavior and on more than a moral scale. As we have seen before, for Lonergan, "You never meet a human being who is not a full human being." And in looking at full human beings, we must look as the fullness of what they express, the history that has made them, the struggles they cannot elude, the self-deceptions it would be difficult for them to do without, the wounds they carry with them, and the world in which all of this takes place.

5

Lonergan and Philosophy: Taking Stock

In this final chapter, I would like to step back from the specifics of Lonergan's work in order to ask about his relationship to philosophy more broadly. But before that, let's take a look back at the themes we have canvassed in order to see their engagement with one another. The refutation of Nietzsche's aphorism, the depictions of self-deception, and the presentation of normative complexity are not isolated from one another. As we have seen periodically throughout, there are relationships among them. If we pause over them a moment outside their embeddedness in the characters and plots in Lonergan's films, we can see this at a more general level.

First, what wounds us without killing us will often tempt us into self-deception. Tragedies happen that we are involved in one way or another, whether by our participation in causing them or simply by suffering them. Or perhaps they aren't tragedies; there are many situations that challenge our sense of who we are or behaviors we exhibit that throw us back on ourselves. Whatever they are, they may involve things that are difficult to cope with. We are not equal to them. This can be disorienting, a disorientation that can express itself in any number of ways, but often accompanied by anxiety. That anxiety, in turn, pushes us away from the situation and perhaps from ourselves. Rather than confronting the situation we instead seek to take cover. We shut down in one way or another and so fail to see what we are about. If we look at all, it is somewhere other than at ourselves.

This, as we have seen, is not always a problem. We may, if we're in a particularly masculine frame of mind, see the very fact of self-deception as a weakness. Often it is, and sometimes it needs to be confronted. But at other times it is necessary for our psychological survival. For the vast majority of us, admitting to ourselves all of our flaws, all of what makes us or has the potential to make us unequal to certain situations, would be too much to bear. Self-deception is a necessary aspect of who we are. And it is expressed with particular force in those situations to which we are not equal but which it would kill us to admit our inequality. Among these, death, however encountered, is central.

Self-deception in turn is bound up with our normative complexity. On the one hand, there are values we cannot live up to, and central to these are moral values. This is because moral values are often more deeply embedded in our sense of who we are than other types of values. Which values are the moral ones may to some extent be a cultural matter. However, values that we call moral ones as we look out not only on our culture but also on others are the ones that are often considered the most egregious ones to violate.[1] It is not incumbent on us to be spontaneous or adventurous or to bring beauty into the world; if we are callous or cruel or hypocritical, however, that's a problem. In the face of our failure to live up to moral values, then, self-deception becomes a temptation. To be sure, in keeping with the character of self-deception, it is a temptation we cannot be aware of ourselves. Rather, it is a temptation to which we give in, if we do so, without our even knowing it.

In addition to our failures to live up to certain values leading us toward self-deception, self-deception can often lead us toward other values. Perhaps it is because we are not strong enough to confront an egregious injustice or even face our failure to be good parents that we throw ourselves into other projects, projects that may have their own worth and engage us in expressing different values. An adolescent withdraws from the social situation at her school because she cannot confront her peers on their racism toward others and takes up an instrument in order to join a band. Gradually music becomes an important part of her life and she dedicates herself to its expression. A man in a loveless marriage begins to train for marathons just to be out of the house. He becomes dedicated to his running, and through his failure to confront his personal situation displays an intensity of athletic involvement that he would otherwise have been unable to muster. Self-deception, then, does not only provide refuge from our deficiencies. It also may foster strengths on a different normative register.

Finally, what does not kill us but does not make us stronger is also related to our normative complexity. If our living were only to be measured on one scale, that of our strength, then most of us would fall short much of the time. In particular, we are rarely entirely equal to the deep tragedies that beset us. We bear our wounds not as battle scars in a war in which we are winners but instead as marks of a history we will never entirely overcome. We are not simply combatants in a series of challenges any more than we are actors in a drama that is to be judged entirely in moral terms. What we saw of morality in the previous chapter is just as true of strength in the second chapter. While there is often merit in strength, there is more than that to being human, and there are other things to be admired, emulated, or appreciated, than our expression of it.

The interaction of the three themes that have been under discussion here reinforces the idea of human complexity. To say that we never meet a human being who is not a full human being, and not only to say it but to grasp it in its force, is to recognize that there is often more going on—and rarely less—than meets the initial glance. Those around us, even those immediately around us, are comprehensible to us to one degree or another, but we need to recognize that we rarely "capture" them as they are. Their history and their struggles, to one degree or another, elude us. We may occasionally judge them—and rightly so—for what they have done or failed to do. We may find them lacking in moral character or worthy of fault in moral action, or we may find them to be weak when strength is required of them. However, we must always bear in mind two things. First, for almost all of them, our judgment does not capture everything that is salient about them. Except perhaps for the most evil people, others cannot be reduced to a single scale of judgment. Second, we are likely unaware of some of the saliences that our judgment does not capture. There is more to them than we know, or can know.

We have spoken of self-deception, where people are ignorant of the entirety of who they are. There is another ignorance as well, that of who others are. This other ignorance is not a contingent matter, something we can overcome simply through more knowledge. Rather, it is part of what it is to be a separate human being that another's experience—the way they live their history, the nuances of the perspectives they take up—is never entirely present to one. While it may be that the one who says, "I know you better than you know yourself" is on rare occasions correct, it is probably more often the case that their believing shows that they know themselves less than they think.

Lonergan, Narratability, and Particularity

The Italian philosopher Adriana Cavarero is often critical of the history of Western philosophy. Her complaint is that such philosophy, in its generality, misses much of the human experience. In her book *Relating Narratives: Storytelling and Selfhood*, she speaks of "two discursive registers that manifest opposite characteristics. One, that of philosophy, has the form of a definitory knowledge that regards the universality of Man. The other that of narration, has the form of a biographical knowledge that regards the unrepeatable identity of someone."[2] Of these two discursive registers, it is the second that interests her. She speaks of it as a challenge to philosophy, a challenge to its arrogance in thinking it can reduce human experience to the categories it proposes.

For Cavarero, it is not only storytelling that reveals this to us, although we will return to that in a moment. There are other indicators as well. One of them, discussed in *For More Than One Voice: Toward a Philosophy of Vocal Expression*, is the materiality and particularity of the human voice, most powerfully instantiated in the mother's voice to her infant child. In focusing on the semantic character of language, philosophy neglects the unrepeatable character of the voice in which language is given. "The philosophical tradition does not only ignore the uniqueness of the voice, but it also ignores uniqueness as such, in whatever mode it manifests itself. The unrepeatable singularity of each human being, the embodied uniqueness that distinguishes each one from every other is, for the universalizing tastes of philosophy, a superfluity."[3]

Cavarero herself sees this critique as a feminist one. For her, the categories to which philosophy in its history has reduced human experience are those of Man. The materiality and particularity eschewed by philosophy are, for her, associated with women's experience and have for that very reason been sidelined by the male project of philosophy. I will leave aside the question of whether the philosophical neglect she cites is a sexist one and (except for a parenthetical remark below) whether the problem is philosophy itself or the way in which it has been done.[4] Rather, I want to focus on the particularity in which she is interested, specifically the particularity she sees in stories.

For Cavarero, our lives are not stories. We do not live stories. This means at least two things. First, there is no script that we consciously follow. We don't ask ourselves what our next lines are or what we are meant to do from here. Second, and less obvious, there is no underlying script that directs us. We aren't expressions of a story that preexists our living, one that might be discovered through self-reflection or perhaps a practice like psychoanalysis. However, this does not mean that stories have nothing to do with our lives. If our lives are not narrations, they are what she calls *narratable*. "[I]n personal experience, the narratable self is at once the transcendental subject and the elusive object of all the autobiographical exercises of memory."[5]

We might put Cavarero's point this way. Although lives themselves are not stories, they can be "storified"—they can be made into stories. The chronological structure of lives is such that they can be narrated in the form of stories. Recognizing this, however, involves also recognizing that there isn't a single story that must be told about a life. There can be many different stories that are equally good, that equally weave together the facts of a person's life into a coherent whole. Not every story will do—the facts of a person's life constrain the character of the stories that can be told. But neither is there a single underlying story that lies there awaiting telling.

Alongside this idea that lives are narratable rather than pregiven narrations or stories is Cavarero's claim that often we don't tell ourselves the stories of our lives. Instead, they are told to us. There are some stories we cannot tell, such as the story of our birth. Other stories we cannot tell because we are ignorant of aspects of ourselves (consider self-deception an example of this) or because we cannot see ourselves as others see us. It's not that we don't tell stories about our lives. We do that all the time, often in small ways. Rather, it's that narratability opens out on to more than a first-person endeavor. Our narratability is a social condition, not just a personal one.

Cavarero illustrates this second personal aspect of narratability throughout *Relating Narratives*, but one striking example is that of Oedipus. There is a crucial aspect of his life of which Oedipus is not aware: the circumstances of his birth. In coming to learn these from the shepherd, he comes to learn other facts—his killing his father and marrying his mother—that create a different story from the one he had told himself over the course of his life up until these facts became known. He learns about himself from another, and specifically from the story told to him about who he is from that other person. The stories that Oedipus had told himself about himself, based on what he knew, were not necessarily wrong. Rather, they were incomplete. Another story could be told about him, but it had to be told by someone else.

Moreover, the particular story that Oedipus is told helps contradict Oedipus's more universal account of Man in his answer to the riddle of the Sphinx. Oedipus, it will be recalled, was posed the riddle that he had to answer in order to continue on his journey to Thebes. The riddle the Sphinx poses is, what walks on all four feet in the morning, two in the afternoon, and three in the evening? Oedipus answers that it is Man, who crawls in infancy, walks as an adult, and uses a cane when he gets old. As Cavarero points out, this is a universal definition of Man. It fails to see individual people and their stories, effacing them in a general philosophical definition that answers to the general philosophical question, What is Man? Oedipus's learning his own story, among other things, undercuts that general philosophical approach. It does not do so by refutation, which after all would probably still be at a general philosophical level, but rather by pointing to the particularity that is Oedipus's life.

In this contrast between the general and the particular, Cavarero insists that our lives are characterized by particularity and that the neglect of that is an offense to those lives. Moreover, that particularity lies, among other places, in the particular narratability of each of them. (It also lies, as her book on the voice insists, in the particular materiality of our voices.) Cavarero posits a "confrontation between two discursive registers that manifest opposite characteristics. One, that of philosophy, has the form of a definitory knowledge that regards the universality of Man. The other, that of narrative, has the form of a biographical knowledge that regards the unrepeatable identity of someone … . Oedipus is implicated in both questions, but it is obviously the latter that occupies the scene of *Oedipus the King*."[6]

Lonergan's films do not state, as Cavarero does, that people have unrepeatable biographies. Strictly speaking, they do not even show it, as in demonstrating it. That would involve somehow using the cinematic medium to make a general statement about human beings, a trick I'm not sure that the medium as such could pull off. (For those who think that Cavarero's claim that people have unrepeatable identities is a universal one, and therefore is in contradiction to her own criticism of philosophy—I agree. Cavarero, it seems to me, has not offered so much a critique of philosophy itself as much as a critique of some of its more tenuous approaches.) What his films do instead is offer glimpses into the lives of specific people in ways that allow their particularity to become evident to us. He shows us people in their fullness, and the fuller they are the less likely they are likely to be repeatable. There have undoubtedly been many people who, through the death of their parents, have held their emotions in check through conforming to the social norms around them. Among those, there are surely some—probably also many, but fewer than the previous group—who have gone through wilder periods in their younger years only to suppress them as they grew older. But how many of them live their constraints with the smile that Sammy Prescott does? And among those, how many are drawn out of themselves by a maddening wayward brother whose absence is always a source of loss and sleep with their boss and protect their son the way she does? How many exhibit the particular way she does of neither being killed nor strengthened or of deceiving herself or exhibit her particular normative complexity? In building the intricacy of his characters—as well as his actors displaying them the way they do—Lonergan offers us particular lives that *invite us* rather than *argue* for thinking of them in their specificity and unrepeatability.

For Cavarero, this unrepeatability is linked to narrative. It is the biographical details of a person's life that resists philosophical universality and offers us a particular person in her uniqueness. It might seem that Lonergan's films do the same thing, since, it might be claimed, they are also narratives of people's lives. Especially in his films, which work through unfolding situations in which people come to deal with difficulties they are confronted with, it could seem that it is precisely through complex narratives that their unrepeatability emerges.

I think, however, that this is a mistake. It is so largely because fictional cinema, I believe, is not a narrative in the same way that a biographical story is. When someone tells a biographical story, there is only the story there and nothing else. The identity of the person given in the story is constrained by the limits of what is said. This does not mean that the story itself claims that the person is reducible to the story. When Oedipus is told the story of his birth (just that story, not the play as a whole), the story itself does not say that Oedipus is nothing other than the killing of his father and the marriage to his mother. It says something about who he is, but does not preclude saying other things about who he is. As the critic John Berger noted in his novel *G.*, "Never again shall a single story be told as though it were the only one."[7]

Fictional cinema, as well as theater, does not tell a story in the same way. (I leave aside here the question of documentary cinema, whose constraints are closer to those of biographical stories, as well as experimental and other forms of cinema.) Rather, it shows a series of events (not, as we have seen, necessarily in chronological order) that display what people are doing and sometimes, through their doing, what they are thinking and feeling. However, it does not have the kind of delimiting frame that a told biographical story does. It does not exhibit the kind of constraints that telling a person a story about who they are must conform to. In that way, cinema might be said to wear its narratability on its sleeve more than a biographical story does. There are many adequate stories that can be told about a character based on what one sees of them in a film, the more depending on how richly the character is drawn.

It may be argued here that stories, especially if they are nuanced in the way a good novel is, do the same thing. After all, novels leave themselves open to different interpretations, and are there not richly drawn characters in novels that can be seen from many distinct angles, angles that would offer us their unrepeatability—or at least particularity—in the same way that films do? I believe the answer to this question depends on the structure of the novel. If the novel is more biographical in structure, then it will be closer to biographical stories than to fictional cinema of the kind Lonergan creates. However, novels take many different forms and I don't want to argue that all of them, even though they are constructed in from words, have the same character as biographical stories. My comparison here is a more limited one. It is between, on the one side, fictional cinema of the kind we have seen with Lonergan rather than cinema in general and, on the other side, biographical stories of the kind Cavarero discusses rather than linguistic (or even novelistic) creation in general. In this comparison the difference lies in the fact that the stories are told and the films don't so much tell us things as show us things that can be told in different ways. (Of course some fictional films, like some plays, have off-screen narration, but those are reversions to standard storytelling. If that were all there was to a film, it would not actually be a film.)

To the extent that this is true, films like Lonergan's are even better exemplars of narratability than a story or even a set of stories told to someone by someone else (or, for that matter, stories people tell themselves about themselves). This is not because he set out to exemplify narratability. Rather, it is because the particular genre of film in which he works displays narratability in a way that is unavailable to a biographical story. We might say that fictional cinema happens at a level beneath a given biographical story; it is the narratable material out of which stories are constructed, much as people's lives are the narratable material out of which the particular stories discussed by Cavarero are constructed. And because of the complexity of Lonergan's characters, that narratability is underlined. They offer the audience, as we have seen, many angles from which to construct stories about them.

What about the second personal nature of storytelling that Cavarero discusses? For her, the narratives that tell us who we are largely come from others, as the story of the shepherd telling Oedipus about his birth illustrates. It is not only birth stories, of course, that come to us from others. We are, as Cavarero insists, actors in a world in which others see us and so are positioned to tell us stories about ourselves. "Even before another can render tangible the identity of someone by telling him/her his/her story, many others have indeed been spectators of the constitutive exposure of the very same identity to their gaze. In other words a human being, in so far as he/she is unique and shows him- or herself to be such from the time of his or her birth, is *exposed*."[8] This exposure should not be taken to be a mark only of vulnerability. For her, people desire to hear their stories, to be given a sense of who they are through them. She uses as a case in point, among others, Ulysses weeping in recognition of what he has accomplished when, as an unrecognized guest in the court of the Phaeacians, he hears the story of his exploits sung by a blind rhapsodist. While I'm not sure this is the case with everyone—or the case with every story that might be told to a person—Cavarero is surely right in maintaining that our exposure to the world allows others to tell us stories about who we are to which we would not have access without their telling us.

Here the situation with Lonergan's characters is different. The events undergone by the characters in his films are exposed to us, the audience, rather than to them. While they might tell stories to one another as when, at the end of *Count*, Terry recalls for Sammy what they used to say to each other when they were kids in order to remind her of the nature of their relationship, the narratable events that we see in the films are given to us, and we are unable to form them into stories to tell the characters themselves. We can come to understand aspects of the characters' identities as we interpret them by telling their stories to ourselves or one another, but we are barred from offering them the solace Cavarero associates with a person's hearing her own story told to her. I suspect this fact has something important to do with some of the emotions people experience in watching Lonergan's films—emotions that run deep for the viewer but must remain out of conversation with the characters. However, I will leave this elusive topic to the side since it would bring me into aspects of film theory and the philosophy of emotion that are far outside my ken.

Lonergan and Cinema

The philosophy of film is a growing field in the arena of philosophical studies, and I am, as I mentioned in the acknowledgments, no expert in it. However, it would be good to close this book with some concluding general reflections on the place of philosophy in Lonergan's films. These will necessarily be broad and speculative, given my limitations in the field; I hope they will stand more as invitations to further conversation rather than settled pronouncements on the issues. We have already seen Lonergan's relevance to specific areas of philosophy in the three preceding chapters; so let us now, if one can abide the metaphor, pull the lens back and take at least a cursory look at his philosophical place more broadly.

In a helpful article entitled "Recent Work on Cinema as Philosophy," Paisley Livingston has botanized several different positions one might take regarding the philosophical character of cinema. The strongest claims he associates with what he calls the "bold thesis:" "films can make independent, innovative and significant contributions to philosophy by means unique to the cinematic medium (such as montage and sound-image relations), where such contributions are independent in the sense that they are inherent in the film and not based on verbally articulated philosophizing, such as commentary or paraphrase."[9] He associates the bold thesis with film theorists whose work derives from the monumental two-volume treatment of cinema by the philosopher Gilles Deleuze.[10] The bold thesis would assert that cinema can make philosophical contributions that traditional philosophy cannot because of the structure of the cinematic medium. Moreover, those contributions would be impossible to translate entirely adequately into verbal philosophy because of their special nature. It might be possible for traditional philosophy to talk about what films are doing philosophically, but it would be barred from actually doing it.

Livingston expresses skepticism about the bold thesis. He writes,

> If we are in doubt whether a film expresses or contains such valuable philosophical content, it would seem reasonable to ask for an independent articulation of it; should such a request be met, that content's putative dependence upon a uniquely cinematic form has been betrayed; yet if the request is not met, there remains reasonable doubt as to the very existence of the innovative and purely cinematic philosophical content.[11]

For Livingston, the dilemma faced by the bold thesis is grounded in his view that philosophy must have content that can be reflected on, criticized, extended, and so on. In addition, it must be able to say what that content *is*. If cinematic contributions to philosophy cannot be rendered verbally it would be impossible to do this, and so it would be impossible to say whether a philosophical contribution has been made. Alternatively, if it would be possible to render the contribution verbally, then cinema's contributions to philosophy would not be unique to cinema.

It is difficult—at least for me—to imagine what an example of a uniquely cinematic contribution to philosophy would be. In any event, it's not clear that, even if it were possible, it is to be found in Lonergan's films. As we have noted, his films are largely dramatic, a fact that stems from his previous (and current) involvement with the theater. To be sure, there are aspects of his films that would be difficult to render on a stage, for instance the sweeping hillside view of the parents' graveyard that nearly bookends *Count*. However, Lonergan is not an experimenter with the cinematic medium, and because of this it is unlikely that we would find a peculiarly cinematic attempt to render a philosophical point.

A second, weaker thesis focuses on the director or filmmaker, claiming that it is they who are doing philosophy through their films. Films express philosophical viewpoints, those of their authors, in much the same way a philosophical text may be said to express the viewpoint of its author. This position is articulated, among others, by Thomas Wartenberg, who, Livingston writes, "wisely concedes that saying a film 'does philosophy' is only a 'shorthand expression for stating that the film's makers are the ones who are actually doing philosophy in/on/through film.'"[12]

Livingston raises two doubts about this view. The first concerns authorship. While it is easy to locate the author of a traditional philosophical text, it is more difficult to do so in a film. There are many contributors to a film, from producers to technicians to actors. It is often hard to locate the particular contribution of, say, the director to a film and therefore to say what cinematic expression is coming from the director and what is coming from others. Second, there is a problem of evidence. Without a director's saying what they are seeking to express, how do we know that what we're interpreting philosophically is actually a product of the director's intention? "The audio-visual evidence," he writes, "underdetermines the initial choice of philosophical propositions, so the interpreter's selection of philosophical background sources is insufficiently motivated in the absence of additional background evidence pertaining to the filmmaker's *actual* sourced and attitudes."[13]

In Lonergan's case, I don't think the first doubt is nearly so damaging to such a view of doing philosophy through film. It is clear that he is in charge of the set and that his actors defer to him. This is not to say that he doesn't respect the actors themselves. But they trust and follow his lead, as the scene with Casey Affleck and the bag of groceries illustrates. It seems to me reasonable to say that what is getting expressed through his films is largely, if not completely, what Lonergan means to express. This point is underlined by the controversy around *Margaret* discussed in the first chapter. Lonergan has visions for his films and, as that controversy displayed, he does not readily give up those visions in the face of criticism or even financial strain.

Moreover, it is easy, I believe, to overstate that first doubt in comparison with philosophy. As those who have written philosophy know, the voices of other philosophers are often ventriloquized—sometimes unconsciously—in one's own writings. This ventriloquism can appear both in the thoughts expressed as well as in the phrasings themselves. I have been struck sometimes to notice that something I've said has already appeared in someone I have read, requiring me to go back and place an extra footnote or even quotation around a thought I had considered my own.

Regarding the second doubt, the evidential one, matters are a bit trickier in Lonergan's case. He has not, to my knowledge, stated many of what could be called "philosophical" intentions in the creation of his films. And we have here good evidence of his intentions at least in two of the three films where there are voice-overs. However, there are some elements of the films that he does give a broadly philosophical tint to. Two of these stand out. The first is his voice-over claim from *Manchester* that this book has often invoked: "You never meet a human being who is not a full human being." While that statement is a minimal one in terms of content, its development across his films has led to some of the complexities we have discussed here. The richness of Lonergan's characters, a richness that he means to achieve, has led to some of the philosophical expressions that his films offer.

This does not mean that Lonergan necessarily sought to offer the particular philosophical expressions that we have interpreted here. That seems unlikely. The closest his claim about a full human being comes to the philosophical issues we have discussed here is its similarity to Cavarero's insistence on the uniqueness of human beings as revealed through the narratives of their lives. And indeed there is a closeness here. However, there are a couple of differences worth noting. First, although this may be a bit overly precise, fullness is not the same thing as uniqueness. Although the fullness of Lonergan's characters does give each of them a unique sensibility, what Lonergan is after in the citation is the richness of the characters themselves, not the uniqueness relative to one another that is Cavarero's concern when she speaks of narratability.

Second, as we have seen, the uniqueness displayed by (as opposed to claimed for) Lonergan's characters does not arise simply from the narratives that are told about them, since no narratives are actually told about them. Rather than being the subject of narratives, they display their uniqueness through the narratability that each film lends to them through the way fictional cinema operates, a way of operating that Lonergan uses to great effect.

It is also doubtful, to use a second example, that the normative complexity that contrasts moral with narrative values was intended by Lonergan. He certainly meant to show us different sides of, say, Terry Prescott. But it is unlikely that he meant to display the particular philosophical conflict I have argued appeared through Terry's character in *Count*. However, by presenting Terry as a full human being, he opens the possibility for that philosophical conflict to be expressed through his character.

The one place we might see intention animating a philosophical expression in Lonergan's films is in regard to self-deception. As we have seen, Lonergan was, as he put it, "raised by the New York Psychoanalytic Society." That would certainly open out onto the possibility of authorial intentions regarding the self-deception of some of his characters. And we have seen that self-deception in play. However, I have argued that the self-deception they display sits ill with a traditional psychoanalytic interpretation. For instance, the socially grounded nature of self-deception discussed by Michael Billig and exemplified by Sammy and Terry's relation to Scottsville as well as Lisa Cohen's relation to Monica Patterson's death is distant from the explanation of the phenomenon offered by Freud. They show how self-deception often arises, not from childhood conflicts within some anthropologically grounded family drama, but instead from the engagement of one's history with the norms of one's social context.

If cinema does not philosophize through its own unique medium, and if, at least in Lonergan's case, the films are largely not the expression of philosophical intentions, then how might we think of the philosophical character of his films? Livingston offers a third option, one that he is also skeptical of but I think he underestimates. He calls it fictionalizing. "Another interpretive goal is to fictionalize, that is, to use some text or display as material for one's own creative, philosophically oriented musings … an imaginative and creative reading of the fictional events, performed more in a spirit of invention than a spirit of discovery, can be developed and presented for several different reasons."[14] Among these reasons would be "to use the film to exemplify and illustrate a philosophical position that has already been developed and elaborated in greater detail elsewhere" or "to say something that significantly advances the debate about a philosophical problem (such as skepticism, personal identity, moral dilemmas …)."[15]

Livingston contrasts this fictionalizing with what he calls "*appreciative interpretations*, which have the primary goal of describing a work's meaning in an effort to understand this and other aspects of the film-maker's actual artistic achievement."[16] An appreciative interpretation needs to rest on the creator's actual intentions, and in cinema those intentions are rarely to be found.

I believe the contrast Livingston draws between fictionalizing and appreciative interpretations is a false one. Films can contain meanings or implications that go beyond the intention of their creators. This claim, of course, is rooted in an old debate about the "intentional fallacy," the idea that it is a mistake to ground interpretation of a fictional (or even nonfictional) work on the intentions of the author in creating it.[17] We might take the position that a close reading (and viewing) of Lonergan's films offers philosophical implications that are not simply imposed upon but drawn from the films themselves. In some cases it might need the assistance of previously developed philosophical theory, but that does not mean it's not there to be seen, or, if one prefers a weaker thesis, that it cannot reasonably be found in the film and offers a better interpretation than competing interpretations might be able to manage.

We have already seen this idea in the discussion of Cavarero's concept of narratability. While the concept is hers—it does not rest on Lonergan's intention to utilize it—it allows us to see something that is in play in the films themselves. Moreover—and this is a point of philosophical interest—the films, by allowing us to see her concept concretely embodied in characters' lives, offer a plausibility to her position that goes beyond what her conceptual position alone might allow for. By seeing narratability in action, we can become more convinced of its plausibility than a straightforwardly philosophical argument might accomplish. And it seems that Cavarero herself might have recognized this in her own work, since she uses specific stories such as those of Oedipus and Ulysses to illustrate her point.

If this is true, however, are we led back to the bold thesis already criticized by Livingston? Is cinema doing philosophical work here that cannot be done in the traditional philosophical medium? I think that would be saying too much. The situation is neither one of mere exemplification nor one of philosophical creativity. Rather, it is one of what might be called justification, if we do not take that term in too intellectual a sense. What fictional films (and they are not necessarily unique in this) may accomplish is to introduce a plausibility to a philosophical position that might otherwise be distant from us by remaining to steadfastly on the intellectual register. By showing us how a philosophical claim can operate in people's lives, a film can offer a plausibility to that claim that goes beyond rational or inferential justification. This is not to say that that plausibility itself cannot be the subject of traditional philosophical reflection and discussion. What is shown in a film is not beyond critique. Rather, it is to say that fictional cinema, among other media, can make something resonant for us in a way that would be difficult for traditional philosophy to achieve.

This plausibility is also offered in two of the three other issues this book has discussed, self-deception and normative complexity. In both cases, we have seen previously developed philosophical positions exemplified in Lonergan's films in such a way as to lend those positions a kind of plausibility that they might not have. (This is not to say they wouldn't be plausible as philosophical positions, but rather that there is an extra plausibility evidenced by the films.) This is particularly true of the issue of self-deception. Inasmuch as we see Terry and Sammy Prescott in self-deception, and moreover that that self-deception arises within and is engaged with the social norms characteristic of a small town like Scottsville, the socially grounded interpretation of self-deception offered by Billig becomes more plausible than a traditional Freudian interpretation of repression as stemming from the Oedipal complex. In a more subtle way, Lisa Cohen's self-deception regarding the death of Monica Patterson, before it collapses, reveals the role of social norms in structuring the phenomenon. (One might want to point to her self-deception regarding her father's affection as an example of psychoanalytic repression. But even then, there is nothing in the film to indicate that there is anything particularly Freudian about an adolescent not wanting to admit to herself that her father doesn't care for her very deeply. It can be accounted for in many different ways, all of them converging on the obvious point that kids want their parents to love them.)

We need to be clear here to avoid misunderstanding. It is not that Lonergan's films in any way *argue* that a social interpretation of self-deception is better than an Oedipal one. The films don't argue anything. They show self-deception in action in a particular social context. Moreover, that showing does not deny that there could be other Oedipal elements in the lives of their characters, ones that are not on display in the films. Rather, they offer plausibility to the idea that we cannot reduce self-deception to a traditional psychoanalytic model; social conditions matter for self-deception.

Much the same plausibility is at work in Lonergan's films regarding normative complexity, both within morality and between moral and nonmoral values. Lee Chandler is a morally complex character; he can be neither condoned nor condemned, even if some of his behavior can be subject to moral disapproval. Moral theories that assess or guide our behavior or our living cannot, by themselves, offer judgments of people's moral being. Inasmuch as they are employed to do so they will miss the significance of the history and struggles of the people they are used to judge. *Manchester* doesn't argue for that position, but it gives it plausibility, much as the figure of Terry Prescott gives plausibility to the idea that in judging people moral categories are not enough. If we are to understand and ultimately to come to some assessment of those around us, we need to look at them through a variety of normative lenses. Moreover, as we saw with Lee Chandler's character, we are often likely to be ignorant of those whom we judge. Any judgment of another human being, except in extreme cases, must be not only versatile but also modest.

We have not yet discussed the refutation of Nietzsche's aphorism in terms of plausibility. That is because something different is in play here. Rather than exemplifying or establishing the plausibility of a philosophical position, Lonergan's films work to establish the *implausibility* of the aphorism. While they do not stand entirely as a refutation of the idea that what does not kill one makes one stronger, they offer plenty of reason to think that in many cases that just doesn't happen. Lonergan's characters often carry their wounds with them, adapting their lives to them through self-deception, vulnerability, or some other means. They do not die, but neither are they made stronger through their struggles.

One might want to argue here that in fact the films do stand as a refutation of the aphorism. Inasmuch as Nietzsche might have liked to claim that the aphorism applies to everyone, then to the extent that Terry and Sammy and Lisa and Lee are realistic illustrations of what people can be like, they provide counterexamples to the claim and thereby refute it. However, even this would not be conclusive (assuming that Nietzsche even meant the maxim to apply to everyone).[18] The characters in Lonergan's films, after all, are fictional ones. There is room then to claim that nonfictional characters are more likely to meet Nietzsche's aphorism than fictional ones. Given the realistic and complex way Lonergan's characters have been drawn, that would seem unlikely. However, that is the point. What his characters do is render implausible the judgment that what does not kill one makes one stronger. In that way, they offer the flip side of what we have seen regarding self-deception and normative complexity, displaying the implausibility rather than the plausibility of a certain philosophical position.

So far we have talked about plausibility; films can lend plausibility to philosophical positions. They can do something else as well. They can prompt reflection that would lead to philosophical judgments. In pondering Lonergan's films and the characters in them, we might be led to thoughts that we would otherwise not have had, thoughts that can issue out on to larger philosophical positions. In my own case, the recognition of the falsity of Nietzsche's aphorism was really brought home to me in reflecting on Lonergan's films in a way that I had not considered before. To be sure, I might have come to that recognition in another way. But it was the viewing of the films that brought me to reflection on the aphorism and a confrontation with it.

So then, in the end, how should we respond to the question of whether Lonergan is, through his films, "doing philosophy?" Rather than answer that question, I would like to ask whether it is a well-formed one. The phrase "doing philosophy" is an ambiguous one. I can mean several things, as Livingston has shown. I think there is a better question in the neighborhood, one that admits of more enlightening answer. What, we might ask instead, have Lonergan's films contributed to philosophy? To this question, we might offer several answers.

First, he has offered plausibility to a couple of philosophical positions and implausibility to at least one. He has done so not by taking an explicit philosophical position but rather by showing us lives where we can see plausibilities and implausibilities at work. Moreover, in doing so he has, through the richness of characters he has drawn, provided examples that one does not see in traditional philosophy, examples that go far beyond the impoverished thought experiments many philosophical writings provide. This has allowed us not only to see these plausibilities and implausibilities at work but also more deeply to see them in their complexity and their interrelationship with other aspects of people's character and also—as we saw at the outset of this chapter—in interaction with other philosophical positions.

Second, Lonergan has shown us the folly of several simple philosophical formulations. The depth of our philosophical positions should reflect, or at least not be betrayed by, the depth of the people to whom those philosophical positions are meant to apply. There is a temptation in philosophy, because it often speaks in generalities (a point, as we have seen, that is held up for criticism by Cavarero), to reduce the complexity of human existence in ways that break trust with what one is trying to understand. Exposure to people like the Prescotts, Lisa Cohen, and Lee Chandler can help cure philosophy of this temptation and bring it back to the fullness of human existence, a fullness that philosophical formulations and positions should seek to capture.

Finally, and related, Lonergan's films can promote a certain philosophical modesty, and in fact a modesty that is much wider in application than in philosophy. This modesty is prompted both by his characters and (at least often) in the nature of fictional cinema itself. Because his characters are so many-sided, we should hesitate before coming to a final accounting of who and what they are. This can reflect itself in the philosophical positions we take, but also in our daily lives. Recognizing that we are often in ignorance of people's histories and struggles, we might, in both our philosophy and our personal judgment, craft approaches to the world that are less sure of themselves than we may be normally inclined to. As I write these words, many of us in the United States and elsewhere are living in a period of intense social and political polarization. The kind of modesty Lonergan's films can promote would perhaps offer a welcome restraint on some of that.

In addition, as we have seen, the cinematic aspect of films—that they display lives rather than telling stories—can reinforce this modesty as well as the recognition of the particularity of people's lives. Fictional cinema, at least if it is not too simplistic, illustrates John Berger's maxim that there is never just one story to be told. That itself is a philosophical position, one that is conceptualized by Cavarero under the heading of narratability and amply illustrated by the films we have discussed here.

Thus we should see Kenneth Lonergan not so much as a philosopher but as a filmmaker whose films have philosophical relevance as well as philosophical resonance. He does not make philosophy; he makes films. Those films can speak to us in many ways, among them ways that exemplify, extend, and engage with philosophical positions. And for this we can be grateful, both as watchers of films and as philosophers.

NOTES

1 Introduction

1 https://www.newyorker.com/magazine/2016/11/07/the-cinematic-traumas-of-kenneth-lonergan. This article originally appeared in the print edition on November 7, 2016. (Hereafter, "Cinematic Traumas.")

2 Mead, "Cinematic Traumas."

3 Ibid.

4 Ibid.

5 Ibid.

6 https://www.poetryfoundation.org/poems/44400/spring-and-fall. Accessed August 26, 2018.

7 Mead, "Cinematic Traumas."

8 Friedrich Nietzsche, *Twilight of the Idols, or, How to Philosophize with a Hammer*, trans. Richard Polt (Indianapolis, IN: Hackett, 1997), p. 6. Nietzsche uses the latter half of the aphorism again in *Ecce Homo*, expanding it thus:

> What is it, fundamentally, that allows us to recognize *who has turned out well*? That a well-turned-out person please our senses, that he is carved from wood that is hard, delicate, and at the same time smells good. He has a taste only for what is good for him. His pleasure, his delight cease where the measure of what is good for him is transgressed. He guesses what remedies avail against what is harmful; he exploits bad accidents to his advantage; what does not kill him makes him stronger.

Friedrich Nietzsche, *On the Genealogy of Moral and Ecce Homo*, trans. Walter Kaufman (New York: Vintage, 1969), p. 224. Here the phrase seems to apply not to everyone but only to people who have "turned out well." However, in *Twilight* the maxim appears to be more general in its application, and it has often been taken in its more general sense. In this book we will stick with the more general application of the maxim, regardless of what Nietzsche might have thought. Moreover, in at least the case of some characters, such as Sammy Prescott, I would hesitate to say that she did not "turn out well," unless the idea is to restrict the application of that phrase to a very few people (an interpretation, to be sure, that cannot be dismissed in Nietzsche's case).

2 Irredeemable Suffering

1 FriedrichNietzsche, *Twilight of the Idols, or, How to Philosophize with a Hammer*, trans. Richard Polt (Indianapolis, IN: Hackett, 1997), p. 6.

2 On this, see Chapter 1, note 8.

3 In "Cinematic Traumas," Mead notes, although without attributing the phrase to Nietzsche, that "'Manchester by the Sea' burrows into the mind of a man who experiences a trauma that neither kills him nor makes him stronger. Rather, it leaves him maimed."

4 Moreover, as we will see in the conclusion, the idea of a film's "refuting" a philosophical claim is a vexed one.

5 The two classic articles on moral luck are Thomas Nagel's "Moral Luck," in *Mortal Questions* (Cambridge: Cambridge University Press, 2012), and Bernard Williams's article of the same name in his book of the same name (Cambridge: Cambridge University Press, 1982).

6 There is a logical issue here that might give philosophers pause. If we render Nietzsche's aphorism as a conditional, it would read, "If it does not kill me, then it makes me stronger." The first two films have denied the consequent ("it makes me stronger"), which invalidates the conditional. What we're considering here is the possibility of denying the antecedent, which is fallacious. That is to say, to deny that it does not kill me—or, positively, to say that it does kill me—does not refute the consequent—to claim that it does not make me stronger. Nothing can be concluded logically from a denial of the antecedent. And yet, I seem to be considering the possibility that Lee's action did kill him and therefore did not make him stronger. This is close to what I'm considering. The claim I'm considering is more or less that since Lee's action did kill him we should not expect him to be made stronger by it. Although logically fallacious if we read Nietzsche's aphorism as a

conditional, it seems to me psychologically correct to say that if a person is defeated by something, it will not make him or her stronger.

7 Bryan Stevenson, *Just Mercy: A Story of Justice and Redemption* (New York: Spiegel and Grau, 2014), p. 17.

3 Self-Deception

1 Mead, "Cinematic Traumas."

2 Discussions of repression appear throughout Freud's work. One good short overview of them is in his 1915 article "The Unconscious," reprinted in *General Psychological Theory: Papers on Metapsychology* (New York: Macmillan, 1963), pp. 116–50.

3 "[W]e now assert on the findings of psychoanalysis that a mental act commonly goes through two phases, between which is interposed a kind of testing process (censorship). In the first phase the mental act is unconscious and belongs to the system Ucs: if upon the scrutiny of the censorship it is rejected, it is not allowed to pass into the second phase: it is then said to be 'repressed' and must remain unconscious. If, however, it passes this scrutiny, it enters upon the second phase and thenceforth belongs to the second system, which we will call the Cs." Freud, pp. 122–3.

4 See Jean-Paul Sartre, *Being and Nothingness*, trans. Hazel Barnes (New York: Washington Square Press, 1993), chapter 2.

5 Herbert Fingarette, *Self-Deception* (Berkeley: University of California Press, 1969/2000), p. 41.

6 Fingarette, *Self-Deception*, p. 62.

7 Ibid., p. 72.

8 Alfred Mele, *Self-Deception Unmasked* (Princeton, NJ: Princeton University Press, 2001), pp. 26–9.

9 Mele, *Self-Deception Unmasked*, pp. 28–9.

10 Michael Billig, *Freudian Repression: Conversation Creating the Unconscious* (Cambridge: Cambridge University Press, 1999), p. 54.

11 Billig, *Freudian Repression*, p. 187.

12 Mead, "Cinematic Traumas."

13 Fingarette, *Self-Deception*, p. 72.

14 Ibid., p. 73.

15 Mele, *Self-Deception Unmasked*, p. 97.

4 Normative Complexity

1 I expand on this distinction, adding a third more recent question (Who can I be?) in the first chapter of *Gilles Deleuze: An Introduction* (Cambridge: Cambridge University Press, 2005).

2 Perhaps the most influential recent statement of this position is Bernard Williams's *Ethics and the Limits of Philosophy* (Cambridge, MA: Harvard University Press, 1985).

3 Aristotle's major statement of his ethics is in the *Nicomachean Ethics*, which has been published in numerous editions over the years. See, for one example, the Hackett edition, 2nd ed., trans. Terence Irwin (Indianapolis, IN: Hackett, 1999).

4 Immanuel Kant, *Groundwork of the Metaphysic of Morals*, trans. H. J. Paton (New York: Harper Torchbooks, 1964), p. 88.

5 Kant, *Groundwork of the Metaphysic of Morals*, p. 61.

6 John Stuart Mill, *Utilitarianism* (Indianapolis, IN: Hackett, 1979), p. 8.

7 One might quibble here that a couple of Aristotle's virtues, like wit or pride, are not moral in the way we have come to think of morality. Fair enough, but the bulk of the virtues are recognizably moral in character.

8 For more on this, see my *A Significant Life: Human Meaning in a Silent Universe* (Chicago, IL: University of Chicago Press, 2015).

9 Susan Wolf, "Moral Saints," *The Variety of Values: Essays on Morality, Meaning, and Love* (Oxford: Oxford University Press, 2015), p. 25.

10 Wolf, "Moral Saints," p. 26.

11 Not everyone would view such a world as impoverished. Probably the most famous philosopher to argue that we should live as morally as possible (with morality being defined as "efficient altruism") is Peter Singer.

See, for instance, his early article "Famine, Affluence, and Morality," https://pages.uoregon.edu/koopman/courses_readings/singer_famine_affluence_morality.pdf. Accessed September 17, 2018. His concept of efficient altruism appears later, in such works as *The Most Good You Can Do: How Effective Altruism Is Changing Ideas about Living Ethically* (New Haven, CT: Yale University Press, 2015).

12 Virgina Held, *The Ethics of Care: Personal, Political, and Global* (Oxford: Oxford University Press, 2006), p. 46.

13 One philosopher who has emphasized the moral importance of seeing another person, really seeing them, is Iris Murdoch in *The Sovereignty of Good* (New York: Routledge, 2001).

14 May, *A Significant Life*, chapter 4.

15 Mead, "Cinematic Traumas."

16 Sartre, Jean-Paul, "Existentialism," in *Existentialism and Human Emotion* (New York: The Philosophical Library, 1957), p. 32.

17 In her article "Murdoch and *Margaret*: Learning a Moral Life," Lucy Bolton argues that Margaret presents us with a "moral fable" in Iris Murdoch's sense, one in which there are no easy moral solutions—a fact that must be experienced in order to arrive at recognition of the complexity of the moral world. "Lonergan's film world confounds such simplistic moral judgement, so that Lisa's moral maze can be seen as creating a filmic moral philosophy along the lines Murdoch describes: a vision of the self-reflection Lisa has to experience in order to come by her own vision of a moral world." *Film-Philosophy*, vol. 21, no. 3, https://www.euppublishing.com/doi/full/10.3366/film.2017.0051. Accessed September 25, 2018.

18 Bernard Williams, "Persons, Character Morality," in *Moral Luck* (Cambridge: Cambridge University Press, 1981), p. 5.

19 Williams, "Persons, Character Morality," p. 11.

20 Ibid., p. 2.

21 See, for instance, *Ethics and the Limits of Philosophy* (Cambridge, MA: Harvard University Press, 1985).

22 Susan Wolf, "Good-for-Nothings," in *The Variety of Values* (Oxford: Oxford University Press, 2015), pp. 76–7.

23 Wolf, "Good-for-Nothings," p. 69.

5 Lonergan and Philosophy: Taking Stock

1 There are complications here that would bring us too far afield to discuss. An example of the difficulty of nailing down the exact role of moral values as opposed to others is illustrated by Philippa Foot in her discussion of Kant's categorical imperative in "Morality as a System of Hypothetical Imperatives," *Philosophical Review*, vol. 81, no. 3 (July 1972): 305–16.

2 Adriana Cavarero, *Relating Narratives: Storytelling and Selfhood*, trans. Paul A. Kotttman (London: Routledge, 2000), p. 13.

3 Adriana Cavarero, *For More Than One Voice: Toward a Philosophy of Vocal Expression*, trans. Paul A. Kottman (Stanford, CA: Stanford University Press, 2005), p. 9.

4 I discuss this issue more fully in "Narrative Conceptions of the Self," in *Constructive Engagement of Analytic and Continental Approaches in Philosophy: From the Vantage Point of Comparative Philosophy*, ed. Bo Mou and Richard Tieszen (Leiden: Brill, 2013), pp. 55–70.

5 Cavarero, *Relating Narratives*, p. 36.

6 Cavarero, *Relating Narratives*, p. 13. For another approach to the unrepeatability of people, see Christopher Grau's fascinating "Love and History," *The Southern Journal of Philosophy*, vol. 48, no. 3 (2010): 246–71.

7 John Berger, *G.* (New York: Pantheon Books, 1980), p. 133.

8 Cavarero, *Relating Narratives*, p. 20.

9 Paisley Livingston, "Recent Work on Cinema as Philosophy," *Philosophy Compass*, vol. 3/4 (2008): 590–603, 592.

10 Deleuze, Gilles, *Cinema I: The Movement Image*, trans. Hugh Tomlinson and Barbara Habberjam (Minneapolis: University of Minnesota Press, 1986), and *Cinema II: The Time-Image*, trans. Hugh Tomlinson and Robert Galeta (Minneapolis: University of Minnesota Press, 1989).

11 Livingston, "Recent Work on Cinema as Philosophy," p. 600.

12 Livingston, "Recent Work on Cinema as Philosophy," p. 593. The citation is from Thomas Wartenberg, *Thinking on Screen: Films as Philosophy* (London: Routledge, 2008), p. 12.

13 Livingston, "Recent Work on Cinema as Philosophy," p. 595.

14 Ibid., p. 596.

15 Ibid., pp. 596, 597.

16 Ibid., p. 597.

17 This was first argued in W. K. Wimsatt, and M. C. Beardsley, "The Intentional Fallacy," *The Sewanee Review*, vol. 54, no. 3 (1946): 468–88.

18 On this, see Chapter 1, note 8 and the opening paragraphs of Chapter 2.

BIBLIOGRAPHY

Special Features in Lonergan's Films (Detailed Filmography in Preface and Acknowledgments)

"Commentary by Director Kenneth Lonergan," Special Features, *You Can Count on Me*, Paramount Classics, 2000.

"A Conversation with Kenneth Lonergan," Special Features, *Manchester by the Sea*, K Films Manchester LLC, 2016.

Other References

Aristotle, *Nichomachean Ethics*, 2nd ed., trans. Terence Irwin. Indianapolis, IN: Hackett, 1999.

Berger, John, *G*. New York: Pantheon Books, 1980.

Billig, Michael, *Freudian Repression: Conversation Creating the Unconscious*. Cambridge: Cambridge University Press, 1999.

Bolton, Lucy, "Murdoch and *Margaret*: Learning a Moral Life," *Film-Philosophy*, vol. 21, no. 3, https://www.euppublishing.com/doi/full/10.3366/film.2017.0051. Accessed September 25, 2018.

Cavarero, Adriana, *For More Than One Voice: Toward a Philosophy of Vocal Expression*, trans. Paul A. Kottman. Stanford, CA: Stanford University Press, 2005.

Cavarero, Adriana, *Relating Narratives: Storytelling and Selfhood*, trans. Paul A. Kotttman. London: Routledge, 2000.

Deleuze, Gilles, *Cinema I: The Movement Image*, trans. Hugh Tomlinson and Barbara Habberjam. Minneapolis: University of Minnesota Press, 1986.

Deleuze, Gilles, *Cinema II: The Time-Image*, trans. Hugh Tomlinson and Robert Galeta. Minneapolis: University of Minnesota Press, 1989

Fingarette, Herbert, *Self-Deception*. Berkeley: University of California Press, 1969/2000.

Foot, Philippa, "Morality as a System of Hypothetial Imperatives," *Philosophical Review*, vol. 81, no. 3 (July 1972): 305–16.

Freud, Sigmund, "The Unconscious," *General Psychological Theory: Papers on Metapsychology*. New York: Macmillan, 1963, pp. 116–50.

Grau, Christopher, "Love and History," *The Southern Journal of Philosophy*, vol. 48, no. 3 (2010): 246–71.

Held, Virgina, *The Ethics of Care: Personal, Political, and Global*. Oxford: Oxford University Press, 2006.

Hopkins, Gerard Manley, "Spring and Fall," https://www.poetryfoundation.org/poems/44400/spring-and-fall. Accessed August 26, 2018.

Kant, Immanuel, *Groundwork of the Metaphysic of Morals*, trans. H. J. Paton. New York: Harper Torchbooks, 1964.

Livingston, Paisley, "Recent Work on Cinema as Philosophy," *Philosophy Compass*, vol. 3/4 (2008): 590–603.

May, Todd, *Gilles Deleuze: An Introduction*. Cambridge: Cambridge University Press, 2005.

May, Todd, "Narrative Conceptions of the Self," in *Constructive Engagement of Analytic and Continental Approaches in Philosophy: From the Vantage Point of Comparative Philosophy*, ed. Bo Mou and Richard Tieszen. Leiden: Brill, 2013, pp. 55–70.

May, Todd, *A Significant Life: Human Meaning in a Silent Universe*. Chicago: University of Chicago Press, 2015.

Mead, Rebecca, "The Cinematic Traumas of Kenneth Lonergan," *The New Yorker*, November 7, 2016, https://www.newyorker.com/magazine/2016/11/07/the-cinematic-traumas-of-kenneth-lonergan. Accessed July 26, 2018.

Mele, Alfred, *Self-Deception Unmasked*. Princeton, NJ: Princeton University Press, 2001.

Mill, John Stuart, *Utilitarianism*. Indianapolis, IN: Hackett, 1979.

Murdoch, Iris, *The Sovereignty of Good*. New York: Routledge, 2001.

Nagel, Thomas, "Moral Luck," in *Mortal Questions*. Cambridge: Cambridge University Press, 2012, pp. 24–38.

Nietzsche, Friedrich, *On the Genealogy of Moral and Ecce Homo*, trans. Walter Kaufman. New York: Vintage, 1969.

Nietzsche, Friedrich, *Twilight of the Idols, or, How to Philosophize with a Hammer*, trans. Richard Polt. Indianapolis, IN: Hackett, 1997.

Sartre, Jean-Paul, *Being and Nothingness*, trans. Hazel Barnes. New York: Washington Square Press, 1993.

Sartre, Jean-Paul, "Existentialism," in *Existentialism and Human Emotion*. New York: The Philosophical Library, 1957, pp. 9–51.

Singer, Peter, "Famine, Affluence, and Morality," 1972, https://pages.uoregon. edu/koopman/courses_readings/singer_famine_affluence_morality.pdf. Accessed September 17, 2018.

Singer, Peter, *The Most Good You Can Do: How Effective Altruism Is Changing Ideas about Living Ethically*. New Haven, CT: Yale University Press, 2015.

Stevenson, Bryan, *Just Mercy: A Story of Justice and Redemption*. New York: Spiegel and Grau, 2014.

Wartenberg, Thomas, *Thinking on Screen: Films as Philosophy*. London: Routlege, 2008.

Williams, Bernard, *Ethics and the Limits of Philosophy*. Cambridge, MA: Harvard University Press, 1985.

Williams, Bernard, "Moral Luck," in *Moral Luck*. Cambridge: Cambridge University Press, 1982, pp. 20–39.

Williams, Bernard, "Persons, Character Morality," in *Moral Luck*. Cambridge: Cambridge University Press, 1981, pp. 1–19.

Wimsatt, W. K. and Beardsley, M. C., "The Intentional Fallacy," *The Sewanee Review*, vol. 54, no. 3 (1946): 468–88.

Wolf, Susan, "Good-for-Nothings," in *The Variety of Values: Essays on Morality, Meaning, and Love*. Oxford: Oxford University Press, 2015, pp. 67–86.

Wolf, Susan, "Moral Saints," *The Variety of Values: Essays on Morality, Meaning, and Love*. Oxford: Oxford University Press, 2015, pp. 11–30.

INDEX

Affleck, Casey 38, 145
Analyze That 3
Analyze This 3, 51
Anna Karenina 17
anxiety 59–62, 65–6, 87, 130
Aristotle 90, 95–6, 120, 123

Bach, Johannes 2
Bentham, Jeremy 92
Berger, John 139, 155
Bergman, Ingmar 2
Billig, Michael 56, 60–2, 68, 79, 81, 147, 150
Broadchurch 1
Broderick, Matthew 4

care ethics, 101, 120
Cavarero, Adriana 133–7, 140–2, 146–7, 149, 154–5
Chandler, Kyle 40
consequentialism 89, 91–2, 95–6, 101, 113–18

Damon, Matt 119
death 8, 13–50, 130
Deleuze, Gilles 143
deontology 89, 91–2, 95–6, 101, 113–17
Dickens, Charles 2
Dou, Gerritt 125
Drnaso, Nick 1

Farhadi, Asghar 1
Fellini, Federico 2

Fingarette, Herbert 56–9, 62, 69–70, 85–6
Freud, Sigmund 10, 53–5, 60, 148

Gallagher, John Jr. 119
Gangs of New York 3
Gilbert, Gary 6
Godard, Jean-Luc 2
The Good Place 1

Hedges, Lucas 40
Held, Virginia 101–2
Hopkins, Gerard Manley 6–7
Howard's End 3

intentional fallacy 149

Janney, Allison 31

Kahneman, Daniel 59
Kant, Immanuel 91, 120, 123

Linklater, Richard 1
Linney, Laura 19, 103–4
Livingston, Paisley 142–9, 153

Manchester by the Sea 2, 5, 6, 12, 17, 73, 146, 151
  and death 8, 17, 38–50
  and normative complexity 105–13
  and self-deception 10, 80–6
Margaret 5, 6, 12, 145
  and death 8, 17, 29–38, 50

and normative complexity 113–21
and self-deception 63–71
Mead, Rebecca 3–7, 51, 63, 110
Mele, Alfred 58–9, 62, 71, 84
Mill, John Stuart 91
Murakami, Haruki 1

narratability, 135–6, 139–41, 149
narrative values 93–4, 103–4, 123, 125
Nietzsche, Friedrich 9, 13, 50, 152
    Nietzsche's aphorism 10, 14, 16, 44–5, 47, 49, 88, 129, 153

O'Brien, Ben 39

Pacquin, Anna 31
psychoanalysis 4–5, 52–5, 118, 134, 147, 151

Ruffalo, Mark 4, 31

Sartre, Jean-Paul 55, 111, 122
Scorcese, Martin 6
self-deception 4, 10, 12, 51–88, 116–18, 121–2, 127, 129–32, 135, 147–8, 150–3

Shakespeare, William 92–3
Smith-Cameron, J. 4, 34
Stevenson, Bryan 49

This is Our Youth 3, 47
Tolstoy, Leo 17
Tversky, Amos 59
twisted self-deception 84

Uriarte, Maximilian 1

virtue theory 89–90, 101

Wallace, David Foster 1
Wartenberg, Thomas 144
Williams, Bernard 121–2
Williams, Michelle 40
Wilson, C. J. 48
The Wire 1
Wolf, Susan 94–5, 124–5

You Can Count On Me 2, 4, 5, 12, 31, 108, 141, 144, 147
    and death 8, 17, 18–29, 50
    and normative complexity 96–105
    and self-deception 72–80

www.ingramcontent.com/pod-product-compliance
Lightning Source LLC
Chambersburg PA
CBHW070338240426
43665CB00045B/2202